M000003536

"Having known Chuck for ove[r]
has wowed audiences with h[is]
and redemption. This is truly a n[ew]
why we make our choices and how they impact our lives. Let Chuck take you
on a journey to a better understanding of ethical choices and consequences."

Betty Garrett, CMP
President, Garrett Speakers International, Inc.

"Everything in your life is a reflection of a choice you have made. EVERY
CHOICE HAS A CONSEQUENCE is invaluable because it reveals how to
achieve different results by making different choices. This book is thought-
provoking, insightful and rich with ideas. It is as practical, readable and
compelling as his other books. I'm sure this will be another classic."

Steve Gilliland
Hall of Fame Speaker and Author of DETOUR, ENJOY THE RIDE,
HIDE YOUR GOAT, MAKING A DIFFERENCE and TURN THE PAGE

"This book is a primer on choices, consequences and the ethics involved
in decision making, and it's as real as it gets. The author speaks
from experience. He shares his journey, the unethical choices he made
and the consequences he paid. Your poor decision making may not lead
to incarceration as Gallagher's did; however, it can lead to living, as the
author describes it in mind sleep, a state of doing things based on habit,
without thinking about what purpose our actions may have. A few of the
lessons learned along the way:
- You can't change what's going on around you until you change what's
  going on within you
- Freedom and responsibility come with a price
- Choices made with integrity yield positive consequences
- We create our own prisons by never trying new things
- You can find people with integrity anywhere you are
- We all have the potential to make bad decisions
- The combination of the three forces – need, opportunity and
  rationalization – creates a solid platform for potential unethical behavior
- positive choices can have extraordinary consequences

This book should be required reading for every business leader. Come to think of it, those leaders should insist everyone read it! The positive takeaway here is that positive choices can lead to extraordinary consequences. Also, that some of life's most important lessons may come from unexpected places."

Lois Creamer
Author of BOOK MORE BUSINESS – Featured in the WALL STREET JOURNAL and FORBES

"Chuck Gallagher intuitively grasps an often-elusive spiritual truth: Our lowest lows and most painful challenges can be seen and used as opportunities to learn, grow and achieve more than would otherwise be possible. He is a shining example of that truth, and in this book he uses his own experiences to offer practical lessons for us all. We're lucky to have his guidance!"

Rev. Ed Townley

"I saw Chuck Gallagher speak at a business conference and subsequently became friendly with him without ever knowing his history. For that reason, I cracked open his new book, EVERY CHOICE HAS A CONSEQUENCE, differently than I might have if I didn't know Chuck. After all, my thought was 'Let me see what my buddy Chuck wrote' instead of asking 'What am I going to learn from reading this book?'

What's more, I was prepared to like Chuck's new book simply because I like Chuck. What I wasn't prepared to do was have my breath taken away. You see, I also approached this book thinking 'Well, that happened to him, but it would never happen to me.' That attitude was judgmental, yes, and not something I'm proud of, but it's the truth.

By the time I was finishing Chuck's words, though, I was in the 'There but for the grace of God go I' mindset. Chuck made it very clear that his problems, while uniquely his, are just a slippery slope away from what you and I might find ourselves caught up in, too. Or, as Chuck says so eloquently: 'Freedom and responsibility come with a price. The choices we make have consequences.'

EVERY CHOICE HAS A CONSEQUENCE is not necessarily my story or your story. But it is a morality tale that all of us can (and should) learn from. Thanks to my friend Chuck for being brave enough to give us an insight into the potential that we all have to do things that we're not proud of. And to show us how to make the right decisions without paying the price he had to pay."

Bruce Turkel
President, Turkel Brands

"This book is a must read for everyone who has a dream and a desire to succeed. It's also a must read for those who simply want to avoid making mistakes they will regret. Chuck Gallagher does a superb job of explaining how all of our choices dictate where we end up. Even the minuscule choices we make on a daily basis can have a profound effect on our lives, as evidenced by Chuck's personal story. Ethics is not only about right and wrong. It is about being true to oneself and creating the destiny one desires. This book is a fast and engaging read that provides a simple strategy to ensure we are going in the right direction."

Ron Karr
Author of LEAD, SELL OR GET OUT OF THE WAY

"We are all in prison in one way or another. For every choice there is a certain consequence. Chuck's no nonsense, straight to the gut, with heart approach is extraordinary. This book should be required reading for any young person to understand the gravity of decision making, for any leader of a corporation considering the next big move, and then realizing it's in the small choices that makes all the difference. Best line of the book, I'll spoil it for you: Choices made with integrity yield positive consequences. That sentence could change the world. It changed mine. Buy and open this book and be not just moved, but moved to action."

Jason Hewlett, CSP, CPAE
Speaker Hall of Fame

"**C**huck Gallagher nailed it! Whether made consciously or unconsciously, every choice has a consequence. This book is an indispensable tool for any company who wants their team to stay on the straight and narrow."

Steve Rizzo
Author of GET YOUR SHIFT TOGETHER and MOTIVATE THIS!

"**C**huck Gallagher's new book, EVERY CHOICE HAS A CONSEQUENCE, is a compelling account of the real-life impact of ethical mistakes. This great read takes the reader behind prison walls and into the depths of contemplating: "Could this happen to me?" This book provides thoughtful insights and a clear plan for personal and corporate action."

Dan Thurmon
Author of OFF BALANCE ON PURPOSE

"**L**ife is a series of Choices, and every single one of them is connected to outcomes, 'Consequences.' We all know this intellectually, but it's what we 'get' emotionally that shapes our behaviors and then our lives. Chuck Gallagher has made some really good and really bad choices, and he walks you through the learning process through his own story. I guarantee you that reading this book will cause you to look more deeply at how and what you choose. It will also help you guide those you love to better patterns, habits and outcomes."

Jim Cathcart, CSP, CPAE
Bestselling Author and Top 1% TEDx Speaker

"**E**VERY CHOICE HAS A CONSEQUENCE will grab you with the first paragraph, and it won't let go until you get to the last page. Chuck Gallagher has written a remarkable book about a fundamental truth: that the choices we make determine the quality of our lives. Chuck's experiences with the consequences of his own choices, both good and bad, ring true for me, and I think they will for you personally and for your organization. I highly recommend this thoughtful, insightful, motivating book as a resource that can truly change lives."

Joe Calloway
Author of BE THE BEST AT WHAT MATTERS MOST

Every CHOICE *has a* CONSEQUENCE

Why People Stray Off the Straight & Narrow and How to Get Them Back on Track

CHUCK GALLAGHER

LifePaths
Publishing

Every CHOICE Has a CONSEQUENCE

Why People Stray Off the Straight & Narrow and How to Get Them Back on Track

© 2018 Chuck Gallagher

Manufactured in the United States of America.

www.chuckgallagher.com

ISBN 13: 978-0-9794610-6-4

This book is dedicated to my wife, Deb, who is so gentle and kind in reminding me that Every Choice has a Consequence and has been supportive in helping me move in the direction of my dreams.

EVERY CHOICE HAS A CONSEQUENCE

TABLE OF CONTENTS

FOREWORD

WHEN CHUCK APPROACHED ME TO WRITE a Foreword for this book, I was hesitant. My wife Mary and I have been teaching for more than 35 years at the University of Santa Monica in programs pioneering the newly emerging field of Spiritual Psychology, and writing a preface for a business book was a bit out of the ordinary. Would any of my earlier experience have anything to do with what Chuck was sharing in this book? And so, I read. Much to my surprise, what Chuck had written was very much in harmony with what we teach at USM.

First and foremost is the recognition that most people perceive the world backwards. We believe that what happens out there determines how we respond – what sense we make of what has happened out there, and thus how we respond. When prison forced Chuck to slow down and literally disconnect from out there, he slowly came to the realization that the truth is actually the other way around – that what we think determines what happens out there.

And thus, Chuck came to understand the power of one's willingness to accept personal responsibility as the true determiner of what happens out there. From our perspective, there is an unhealthy global tendency in the direction of blaming our disturbances on things happening in our lives, or difficult past events, or people we disagree with, regardless of whether or not we even know them. When this tendency becomes extreme, encompassing relatively large numbers of people, the result is a condition we know as war.

Chuck makes it very clear that the only real choice any of us has is our choice in responding to any experience we have in our lives. And, our experience in working with thousands of people at USM has clearly revealed one of the foundational Principles of Spiritual Psychology, which is, "How you relate to the issue IS the real issue." And, as Chuck so clearly puts it, "Every choice has a consequence."

And if it's true that our inner reality determines what we draw to us in our outer lives, doesn't it make sense that, as Chuck says, Choices made with integrity yielded positive consequences.

What would happen if each of us was willing to consider the possibility that whatever is happening out there in the world is not the real cause of our unhappiness. What if the real root of our disturbance was our interpretation of what we observed happening out there in the world, regardless of whether out there meant anything ranging from political turmoil to one's relationship with one's spouse?

And what if more of us learned to implement the process of taking responsibility for our internal upsets regardless of what we think seems to have caused it? What if we decided to take personal responsibility for these inner choices?

One immediate benefit would be that we'd place ourselves in the position of really being able to do something about our level of disturbance regardless of whether anything changed out there. That one change in and of itself would result in someone experiencing an enhanced sense of empowerment. No more playing victim as an excuse for a life that isn't working as well as one would like.

Another benefit in learning to take a greater level of personal responsibility is to realize, since every choice has a consequence, that even the smallest choice to stray off the straight and narrow will result in a compromise of our sense of personal integrity. And once that first breech of personal integrity has occurred, the second is so much easier – and the third – etc.

While it may not seem immediately evident, much less desirable, is that inmates have placed themselves in an environment where they have lots of time to consider such things and hopefully reach conclusions much more likely to improve the quality of their lives upon release – as has Chuck's.

But even more powerful, this book can hopefully assist the rest of us in coming to the same realization earlier and thus positively alter the course of our lives sooner. The bottom line – start today to build upon your sense of integrity based on the willingness to take responsibility for your personal choices. Choose wisely, then sit back and watch your life change more in the direction you'd like to see.

— H. Ron Hulnick, Ph.D.
Author of *Loyalty To Your Soul* and
Remembering the Light Within

PREFACE

THIS BOOK IS ABOUT CHOICES – the choices we all make and the consequences that follow. For most people, the word "consequences" denotes something bad. That's not true. Consequences are just consequences. They are what happens following a choice that we make. I'm living proof that consequences can be both good and bad depending on the choice that creates our outcome.

In my first book, *Second Chances: Transforming Adversity into Opportunity,* I took the time to reflect on a series of choices that created the consequence of federal prison. Let me be clear, that was not a high point in my life. I had both consciously and subconsciously created a series of choices that changed my life forever. Not once did it occur to me that after obtaining my masters in accounting I would be incarcerated for doing something that I knew was unethical and (as we'd say in the south) downright wrong. But there I was in the mid '90s walking myself into a life changing experience and living out the truth of that statement – Every Choice has a Consequence.

Now, over two decades later and having spoken to tens of thousands of people both in the U.S. and abroad, I am living proof of both sides of the Every Choice has a Consequence statement. This book is not a chronicle of my prison experience – that has long past. Rather, it is an insight into what motivates behavior. Why do we make the choices that we make? Is it possible to be more aware when making a choice of the consequences that are destined to follow? Are there patterns to human behavior that lead to our choices? What can we do to create a foundation that allows us to make choices that create positive consequences – consequences that move our lives forward with momentum toward success?

It would be great if making choices – powerful, insightful choices – that produce instant success was easy. It's not! We are constantly bombarded with sensational schemes to gain a great life easily. The sales pitches are crafty. The problem is they prey on the simple patterns of human behavior that can easily lead us to make choices that in the long run are not for our highest good.

Over the past twenty some years I have been blessed to interview scores of people who, for one reason or another, have made choices that yielded consequences that were unanticipated and certainly not desired. In every case, bar none, when all the fluff was removed what emerged was a clear pattern that was identifiable and, if recognized early on, would have created a way to prevent poor choices from ever being made. Don't get me wrong, I am smart enough to know that we can't prevent all poor choices from happening. What is true, however, is understanding the process by which we make choices can empower us to move from the unconscious or subconscious level to one of empowerment by making conscious choices. Choices that create consequences that propel us forward in a manner that brings the success that most desire.

Yes, I reference my experiences often and most importantly an unexpected teacher named Buck! I remember the TV series years ago – Touched by an Angel – and I often think of Buck as my angel. Little did I know that a 5 foot 6 inch African American man – my cellmate in prison – would become a source of wisdom that I connect with to this day. Buck's insights provided the foundation for later learning that has influenced numerous organizations to connect the dots between how we make choices and what can be done to create a positive influence on creating positive empowering choices.

You can get caught up in the story and perhaps miss the point. But I don't think so! There's something fundamental and profound that happens when we learn what motivates our behavior. By accepting responsibility for what happens, both good and bad, we become empowered to take actions that can create incredible success. After all, a convicted felon isn't supposed to be a

Vice President in a public company. But then again, every choice has a consequence.

You can be a victim or a victor. The choice is yours. I choose victor. Join me in this book and let's together find out how.

— Chuck Gallagher

EVERY CHOICE HAS A CONSEQUENCE

Chapter 1

TWENTY-THREE STEPS OUT

IT'S ODD. It's odd how the beginning of one time of life is often the ending of another. Eleven months earlier I was ending my life, as I knew it, to begin a new phase that I neither wanted nor desired. In fact, where I was headed would be, for the most part, one of the worst experiences imaginable – prison. Yet as I lay in my top prison bunk waiting for 10 p.m. lights out, some eleven months after walking in, I knew that in a few short hours a new journey would begin. I would be retracing the same twenty-three steps I took to enter prison. I would be leaving.

Buck, my cellmate, had a way of saying things that, to me, were profound. I had come to call them "Buckisms," and not long after I arrived I began writing them down. Don't know where they came from, as Buck wasn't inclined to read much, but from somewhere Buck came up with the darnedest comments, ones that seemed to reach in and touch my heart.

My last night, as we prepared for lights out, Buck walked up to my bunk, looked at me with piercing brown eyes, and said in an unusually quiet voice, "Chuck, sometimes in life you get knocked down lower than you could ever imagine, so that when your time comes to stand, you can stand taller than you've ever been. Chuck, stand tall for me. Stand tall for us. We're counting on you!"

While I didn't jump up and immediately write down those words, I knew I'd never forget them.

"Lights out!" we heard the guard shout.

As my fellow inmates anticipated another workday, rising around 5:30 a.m. and preparing for the morning count and the trek to the chow line, I put on civilian clothes and got ready for my departure. Breakfasts were nothing to get excited about, though some prison food was actually quite tasty. But I knew this was the last meal in prison I'd consume. Not eating...well, that wasn't an option, as I'd grown so accustomed to the regimen that I couldn't skip it. Prison has a way of doing that – creating unbreakable habits among inmates. As I made this last journey to the chow hall, I wondered whether the simple habits I'd come to know in prison would be easily shaken when I returned to the "real world."

Compared to some other inmates, I hadn't been in prison all that long. But it was easily the slowest time of my life. Eleven months of an active sentence seemed like eleven years. For me, prison was like being in a time warp where one hour is equivalent to three hours. Everything around you was moving at a normal speed, but you felt stuck. Decisions are made for you, and you're left to sit, think, and wait. You either go crazy or fall in line and join the routine. Moving from this experience to a halfway house was at least a step in the right direction. But make no mistake – the halfway house was still prison.

My cellmate Buck was quiet on this morning, knowing that once again he would be forced to disconnect from his "cellie" and, within days, break in another convict as a cellmate. We had grown quite close. Buck, a fairly short and stocky black man some thirteen years younger than me, had become quite the confidant. Our beginning was rocky, but soon we found a bond that's rare to find in life, and we found it in the most unexpected place. Buck was like an angel – a person of amazing integrity who was willing to be vulnerable, allowing for a deep spiritual connection to develop between us. Now, as I prepared to leave, Buck was sad. But he was glad the ordeal that had begun for me on October 2, 1995, was coming to an end.

"Chuck, you know I'm gonna miss you," Buck said as he turned his head away from me, putting on his clothes for his work detail. Men don't want to show emotion, especially in prison. Signs of weakness can be misinterpreted and abused. But Buck had been in long enough and was strong enough not to let that stand in his way. With shirt now tucked in, Buck turned and gave me a hug I'll never forget.

• • •

Being disconnected from everything forces you to think and focus on yourself, assuming you're willing to go there.

• • •

"I know I'll hear from you once you're out," Buck said and kissed me on the cheek. "Gotta go now. The next time I'll see you is when I'm out." And, with that, Buck made his way from the cell, knowing that anything more would just be too much for us both.

In prison, everything became exaggerated, from the way time passed to the experience of thinking. The good part about prison, if you want to consider the good, was that the experience allowed for personal, internal and emotional exploration. The kind that we don't always get the chance to do in the midst of our busy lives. Being disconnected from everything forces you to think and focus on yourself, assuming you're willing to go there. You have the opportunity to work on who you are and who you hope to be. Hopefully, you use that luxury to reflect on your mistakes and improve yourself.

When I arrived at the front door of this prison, I weighed a little over 205 pounds, not including my heavy emotional baggage. But, as I walked out that door, I was leaving at a healthier 175 pounds, and I'd lost the bulk of my inner baggage as well. My clothes were loose, and my soul felt light.

I waited as my release paperwork was processed and wondered what this new world would hold for me. It was anxiety producing. Would things on the outside have substantially changed? How would I be treated? How would I be able to create a new, meaningful life? I was ecstatic about leaving but experiencing trepidation about the change. After all, leaving prison was just a step toward a new life and new freedom. Buck had said to me during one of our prison walks, "A man without a vision more than likely will return to his past." Return to my past, especially this past – the past of prison – was not an option for me. I had a vision. The only thing that clouded my vision was not knowing what was in store on the outside. I hoped that nothing had changed, but I knew that everything had changed, including who I now was.

As a child comes into the world not knowing what to expect, I had entered prison as one person. The person leaving the prison compound was different, though. True, my personality was basically the same, but my understanding of the world had been transformed. Most importantly, my understanding of myself was radically changed. Now was the time to turn a negative consequence into what could become a positive result. At a deep level, I realized that I had the power to choose to make good things happen. At least I knew that I could now sow different seeds.

At the end of eleven months and twenty-three steps was a new beginning. Leaving the confines of regular prison to enter a halfway house was the first step of my journey back into the world. The awe of being placed back into mainstream society, even if that meant finishing my sentence in a halfway house, was inspiring. The loss of freedom, the loss of contact, and the isolation that come from being incarcerated are painful. Those first steps out the door brought heartfelt joy.

Leaving prison on a beautiful August day was amazing. Not too hot, not too cool, and a radiant blue sky above greeted me as the door I had entered what seemed like forever ago was unlocked so I could take my first steps toward my newfound freedom. I was surprised at how much had changed. I saw the world through a new set of eyes and started to ask myself questions. What had I believed was important before I went in? Was it really important? Coming out of prison, were the same things significant? What might have changed, and how had I changed?

Little things, things that most people take for granted on a daily basis, were remarkable to me. The freedom to be able to choose where you were going to eat felt like an indulgence. In prison, you went to the cafeteria and had breakfast, lunch, and dinner because that was part of the daily schedule. Now, I had the freedom to choose what I ate and where I ate it.

Likewise, going to the mall to buy new clothing was a wonderful experience. Actually it was quite amazing – not because I was buying something new, but because I had the freedom to choose what I would buy and what I would wear. Experiencing each of these little choices through new eyes was something I'd never thought about before. And for me – well, I had only been in a short period of time, relatively speaking.

I recall going into Cary Towne Center and stopping for several minutes, thinking of Buck. Here I'd been incarcerated for a bit less than a year, and now I was awed by this simple experience. I wondered how Buck would feel on the outside. He'd been in for six-plus years, and during that time the world went on without his presence, or so it seemed. I suppose there are many prisons we might find ourselves in, many ways to live life while the world goes on without us. Perhaps, for any of us, one of the biggest takeaways we can come to understand is that, no matter what situation we might find ourselves in, we always have a choice. After all, what we choose, how we act, and how we react to life experiences is our choice.

As I reveled in my freedom, thoughts about some of the people I knew in prison washed over me. I wondered how difficult freedom would be for some of those who'd been in prison for years, isolated from the things we take for granted daily. Most people who are incarcerated discover that life after release is very difficult and foreign. For the first time, I understood why.

Sometimes I use the term "mind sleep" to describe my experience of living. In fact, many of us live in a state of perpetual "mind sleep" – a state of doing things based on habit, not really thinking about what purpose our actions have. Before prison, I got up and did all of the normal things people do on a daily basis, but I didn't think about it at all. My mind was asleep.

Prison changed things for me. Yes, there were routines, but prison awakened me to the vast difference an environment can make. I became keenly aware of the impact that choices have on our daily lives. Every choice has a consequence, and prison was just a physical manifestation of one of the consequences of my past choices. The experience of prison gave me a new awareness of the opportunities and choices available to me. I didn't have complete freedom at the moment I was released, but it was more than I had when I went in, and I was no longer in a state of "mind sleep."

In prison, your daily routine is decided for you. Your choice of food is made for you. The clothing you wear is mandatory and, again, chosen for you. You become institutionalized and can easily start to lose the skills you need to function well in society. I'm grateful that in the eleven months I spent in prison, I didn't lose any of these skills, but the experience had a profound impact on me. I appreciate the freedom I have infinitely more now than I ever did before. Perhaps the best way to truly appreciate what you have is to lose it, at least for a time.

Buck made a comment to me one day while we were walking: "You can't change what's going on around you till you change what's going on within you. If you learn anything here, Chuck, that'll be the lesson. Sadly, so many of us here never get it. We think that prison is a place."

As I heard those words, I stopped him in his tracks. "It is a place," I replied. *What else is it?* I thought.

• • •

"You can't change what's going on around you till you change what's going on within you. If you learn anything here, Chuck, that'll be the lesson. Sadly, so many of us here never get it. We think that prison is a place."

• • •

Wise beyond his years, like an old man in a young man's body, Buck stared back at me, saying, "We create our prisons. Don't think for a minute that most of us, in some way, haven't been in our own prisons – prisons like envy, jealously, hatred and abuse. Chuck, this list goes on."

Buck was right in that many of us have created our own prisons based on our self-esteem or the things we tell ourselves or come to believe. The longer you choose to confine yourself to the prison you're in, the more difficult it'll be to feel comfortable when you're finally released.

Whether your prison is emotional or physical, being released or releasing yourself is difficult. You have to want to make good choices, some of which feel quite unnatural. You must be committed to a positive change. You have to believe in your own power. Something like eighty percent of the time, former prisoners return to prison. Is this because they can't make good decisions? Of course not. It's because they don't. It's because they've been programmed to believe they don't have the power to make good empowering choices.

The same holds true for anyone currently imprisoned and institutionalized by their own thoughts and emotions. In order to free yourself and create a different life, it's necessary to intentionally choose different behavior. Releasing the chains that bind you can be painful, and changing your choices will require dedication and work, but if you stick to it, you'll see that it's worth your effort.

Coming out of a physical prison created an opportunity for me to make a different set of choices. Because of the time I was afforded to reflect on what happened as a result of my choices almost a decade earlier, I saw them through a different lens than I did when I went into prison. Now I was determined to make good and honorable choices, ones that would be more empowering for me. After all, I had made a commitment to Buck to "stand tall."

Chapter 2

MORE THAN HALFWAY THERE

A HALFWAY HOUSE IS STILL A TYPE OF PRISON. Sure, you have more freedom, but not a lot more. You're required to go to work daily and notify the halfway house of your location and movements between locations throughout the day. The expectation is that, due to institutionalization, you're more likely to fail than you are to succeed, so they run a tight ship.

Having seen things firsthand, I can honestly say that the system is not designed to rehabilitate. Prison is a business. Its success relies on a steady stream of people to incarcerate. When individuals fail while they're in a halfway house, they are reincarcerated, keeping the flow of inmates moving. In fact, as a group, they're easier to work with because they've been in prison and know the system.

While I was in the halfway house, I saw a fellow inmate's fear and eventual failure. On his last day in the halfway house, he got up to go to work, but instead he went to a convenience store, stuck his finger in his pocket, and held it up. It was considered an armed robbery. He was immediately sent back to prison. He made that choice because he was petrified about getting out of the halfway house. He couldn't grasp the basics of living on his own: How do I pay rent? How do I sign up for utilities? How do I function outside of a world where three meals a day and a place to stay are provided for me? He was not prepared to make the choices necessary to live a full, free life. It was easier for him to live a life in which others conditioned his actions and responses than it was for him to take responsibility for his choices and live free.

Freedom and responsibility come with a price. The choices we make have consequences, so if we fear our own choices or are unprepared to make them, then we often choose what's easiest: allowing others to make choices for us.

In order to transition to a halfway house, I had to have a job. So I prepared myself to reenter the workforce by reaching out to my former employer. I knew they were under no obligation to rehire me, but the seeds I'd planted with a previous manager back in 1991 meant that I would at least be considered for reemployment. That company has what I would call a soul. They had compassion for me and gave me the opportunity to make a living in sales, albeit on straight commission. What I did with that opportunity would be a direct result of the choices I made and the effort I gave.

• • •

Freedom and responsibility
come with a price.
The choices we make
have consequences.

• • •

My employers knew I had a drive to succeed. They knew that the choices I made every day from now on would determine my future in more ways than one. One bad choice, one slip-up, and I'd end up back in prison. They were counting on what I now understood: I wanted to overcome the label "convicted felon," and I wanted to make better choices.

Lest you think that I was hired back into a cushy job just because of my past experience and relationships, know that I was hired into direct sales. I went door to door, cold calling and trying to scrape together a living selling cemetery property. If I didn't sell anything, I didn't eat. In short, failure was not an option, and success wouldn't be easy.

The opportunity to rebuild my life was far too precious for me to fail. I wanted to prove to everyone what I knew deep inside. I wasn't a failure. I was "somebody," and I would be successful again. What I had also come to understand was that success wasn't about money, title, or any other external thing. Success was about the impact you have on someone else's life.

After my release, time continued to fly by – or that was my perception, anyway. Every day had the same twenty-four hours as always, and I was faced with choices and consequences, just as I'd always been before. But now the realities of the consequences of my choices were magnified. Every choice became important, and each one needed to be made with good and honorable intentions. Seemingly insignificant choices, as I had viewed them with past eyes, were significant today. It seemed to me that the big decisions came into focus easier when I took the time to think about and make the daily little choices well.

Sales weren't easy to come by. I didn't inherit a set of contacts or clients. My job was to build my database of potential clients and grow my own book of business. So I went back to basics. Every choice I made would produce a result, and every result would be something I could build on until I reached whatever future I chose to create.

I was inadvertently working a recovery program. One day at a time. One decision at a time. Gratitude was my attitude. I considered each choice carefully, knowing that it had the power to create the circumstances of my present and possibilities for my future.

Nine months after my release from prison to the halfway house, I began to see the manifestation of my careful daily choices. My sales director announced that she wanted to spend more time at home with her young children, leaving her position open. Before she announced her intentions publicly, the regional president contacted me to ask if I felt ready for more responsibility. Would I be interested in taking over the sales director position? I'd been so focused on making good daily choices that I wasn't expecting to be acknowledged for my work performance. But I gratefully accepted the promotion and was determined to continue on my path.

I'd held the sales director role previously and felt prepared to resume it. But I still didn't take it for granted. I continued to focus on what needed to be done each day in order to rebuild my life. At the same time, I began focusing on how to be a good leader so that my sales team could reach their goals and find success as well. If I could become the number one salesperson for the region in the nine months following prison, I knew that I could teach others the simple process of finding their personal success. It was just making choices and decisions one step at a time.

One thing that I've learned about myself is that I'm really very comfortable living in the future. But prison taught me that while dreaming about the future may be fun, today's choices are going to create my day-to-day experience, not dreaming of what might be. Tomorrow is a mystery. It may turn out just as you expect, or it may be radically different. I'm thankful I learned to focus on the present because this sequence of daily choices over several months allowed senior management to regain trust in my ability and in me.

Doing the right things and making sales was not as easy as just putting my head down and working hard. Shortly after I took the new sales job, the area where I worked was hit by a powerful hurricane. Unless I was selling generators or roofing repair, no one wanted to buy from me just now. They all said the same thing, even if they were interested. They needed time to rebuild their lives following this catastrophic event.

I won't deny that I questioned whether my past was making me a victim of nature's wrath. I wondered how I would succeed when there was devastation all around me. But I realized that life is not about luck, and it's not about timing – it's about choices! If I'd given up, I don't know where I would be today. Which is why I'm so glad that I found the conviction to stay focused on making the right choices each day and putting in the hard work that was necessary.

As spiritual beings, whether we like to admit it or not, we create our reality. I believe that, and my story is proof of it. The multitude of choices I made each day following my release from prison created the opportunities I would eventually receive. My abundance and prosperity continued to multiply. Within three months of my reentry into management, I was presented with another promotion – regional manager of two states.

You could never have convinced me that just one year after being released from prison, I would be managing a $6 million sales organization. A clear pattern was beginning to emerge. Choices made with integrity yielded positive consequences. Experience had shown me both sides of the choice issue. When I made choices that lacked integrity or were unethical, the consequences were extraordinarily negative. But when I made a conscious decision to make good and honorable choices, choices with integrity, I experienced positive results far beyond my expectations.

• • •

A clear pattern was beginning to emerge. Choices made with integrity yielded positive consequences.

• • •

We can change our lives. Each one of us has the creative power we need to influence our present and our future. If you think back, you can probably find examples of how your actions and choices created your present situation. I wish I'd understood this concept earlier in my life. Perhaps it would have kept me out of prison.

We all face our individual prisons, though, and many are self-inflicted. The percentage of people who are physically incarcerated is relatively low. Yet we create our own prisons by telling ourselves things that keep us from trying something new, or that keep us in our comfort zone safe from failure and far from success. In short, we build a prison that stops us from reaching our potential.

• • •

We create our own prisons by telling ourselves things that keep us from trying something new, or that keep us in our comfort zone safe from failure and far from success.

• • •

I took twenty-three steps and learned that life is not about the prisons we find ourselves in – real or imagined. Life is about breaking the chains that bind us. It's about changing the way we think so that we can stop imposing prisons on ourselves and thereby achieve growth, insight, and success beyond measure.

One choice I made that I don't regret is the choice to share my story. My life is an open book. Twenty years after leaving prison, I have rejoined the corporate world and have carried many senior titles for several publicly held and private companies. I feel uncomfortable sometimes when I talk about my success following prison. From the depths of my heart, I can tell you that I don't intend to brag, because there's nothing to brag about. There's only a lesson I carry with me each day. The lesson is this: choices dictate results, whether you're an average Joe, the CEO of a major corporation, or even a convicted felon.

Take a little time to consider the following. How is it that people who are well-intended, who know the difference between right and wrong, who understand what ethical behavior is and know how to act with integrity – how could those same people choose to make unethical and potentially illegal choices that could put them into federal prison? Is it possible that literally anyone could make those choices? Could you?

Coming out of prison I recognized the simplicity and the significance of our choices. Often people take for granted just how much choice they have in their daily lives. Nearly everything you do is a choice. Choices can seem simple, especially ones that are mundane, like what to have for dinner. But you see, even that simple choice can lead to a healthy lifestyle or an unhealthy one.

The significance of those choices is what I hope you will focus on in your own life. Look at where you are today. Think of the choices you've made. You chose where to attend college – or whether to attend at all. You may have chosen a spouse. You chose your job. Those are the big things. But you also got to choose how you'd perform in your job and in your marriage. Have you done your best? Have you been unethical or immoral? Choices are significant because the reason you are where you are is choice – specifically, the individual choices you've made. The reason there's even a possibility of you reaching a goal is because you have choices.

Eleven months earlier, I'd taken twenty-three steps in, and as I walked out the front door on my final day as a prisoner, I took twenty-three steps out with a new understanding of choice.

Ask yourself this: Is what you're doing today getting you closer to where you want to be tomorrow? The answer to that question reveals the power of choice.

CHAPTER 3

HOW DID I GET HERE?

MOVING FORWARD SUCCESSFULLY IN LIFE often requires that we look back in order to understand what choices we made that got us to where we are right now. Buck often said, "Let your past make you better, not bitter." And I have to admit, in order to be a better person, the person I knew I was born to be, I needed to make better choices!

Stepping out of prison provided crystal clarity about a number of life truths. As we live, we confront seemingly insignificant choices on a daily basis that don't appear to have meaning or real consequences. What we have for lunch, for example, is insignificant to most of us. The same is true when it comes to telling a "little white lie." Most of us would rather fudge the truth a bit than deal with the consequences of someone hearing what they might not want to hear. When a friend asks, "How do I look?"

and you know they've put on a few pounds and their outfit is a bit too tight, do you tell the truth – "You're looking a bit porky there" – or do you say, "Fine"? Some people are challenged in dealing with the blatant truth, and so we become conditioned to respond in ways that camouflage what we really see or believe.

• • •

When you make a bad choice,
and no one gets hurt or
there aren't any immediate
consequences, it's easy to believe
that nothing will come of it.

• • •

I'll never forget one evening in prison. An inmate known as "Shine" was in a telephone conversation with his girlfriend. From a distance we could hear that part of the conversation was getting somewhat heated, as Shine raised his voice on more than one occasion. But, as his time on the phone was drawing to an end, Shine took on a calmer approach to the conversation, ending it by saying, "You know that I love you and can't wait to see you when you come to visit next month. Me too...love you too."

As he walked around the corner of our cellblock he said, "Damn bitch. I'm so tired of her. All we do is argue.

I can't wait to get out of here and find me a new woman." Believe me, half the unit could hear his displeasure.

I was wobbled by his words and looked at Buck to gain some insight. How could Shine be so callous and unkind? Here was a woman who paid for his collect calls and came to visit him, and all he could do was complain? Shaking my head in disbelief, I must have had a look of "help" in my eyes because Buck, speaking in a low whisper, shared another truth that I knew but had not yet connected with consciously.

"Chuck, we make decisions every day that seem right on the surface but that we know deep down are not good decisions. Shine doesn't want to lose what he has right now as it serves his needs. Yet, when she can't hear, he spouts off and shares the truth of his experience. His dumb choices got him here, and it'll be those same dumb choices, or similar ones, that'll break up his relationship. Mark my word."

Again, Buck was wise. When assigned so little value, it's easy to let wrong choices build upon each other. When you make a bad choice, and no one gets hurt or there aren't any immediate consequences, it's easy to believe that nothing will come of it.

"I sold drugs," Buck said. "I started when I was fourteen, and the only consequence that happened as a result of my choices was I made money. From fourteen to eighteen I sold drugs. Now mind you, I was no drug kingpin. I was just a street punk, but I had more money than my friends who worked at McDonald's for minimum wage. Since nothing happened as a result of my street corner sales, I believed I was bulletproof."

"So what happened, Buck? Why are you here serving a ten-year sentence?" I asked.

"The more I sold without being caught, the more I thought I was invincible. I just thought there was never going to be a consequence. I was too insignificant for anyone to care. Reality was, however – and I didn't know it – I was being watched by law enforcement for years. You see, if they had arrested me before I turned eighteen, I would have been considered a juvenile offender and got a light sentence. I was arrested two days after my eighteenth birthday, and I got ten years!"

I recall hearing Buck share those words with me, and it struck me many times afterward that it's so easy to get lulled into thinking our choices have no meaning, especially if there's no clear consequence that quickly follows. Buck's choices and, frankly, those of my own that led me to prison, were perceived as actions with no moral code attached to them. The problem is, whether we acknowledge it or not, there's still wrong and right, and every choice has a consequence.

As I walked out of prison, I thought about what had brought me to that place. What was the pivotal moment that turned me into a convict? The answer is that it wasn't a specific moment, but a series of small wrong decisions,

• • •

"What you don't know won't hurt me."

• • •

which I easily dismissed as benign until together they paved the way to my destruction.

The first step on the slippery slope of unethical choices happened in January of 1987. I received a phone call then – one I'll never forget.

"Chuck, this is David at the bank."

"Hi, David. Good to hear from you." As I heard David's voice I suspected that he was sending me yet another client. David worked for NCNB, and we both attended the same Sunday school class and had become business friends. As a result, David was kind in referring clients my way.

"Chuck, is there a problem? Our records show that you're two months behind in your house payment."

As I heard David's words, a chill ran up my spine. What David said was true. My role in the community was that of a financial leader, yet I lacked the discipline and common sense to effectively manage my own money. Up to this point, though, I'd kept it hidden. No one knew, not even my wife. And frankly, I preferred to keep it that way. I guess I lived by the old adage, with a new twist: "What you don't know won't hurt me."

Now, however, I'd been challenged. What to say? I could have told the truth, which would mean admitting that I had not managed my money well. *Hmm,* I thought, *admitting that would most certainly be embarrassing and, more importantly, reduce the likelihood that he would send me more business. Can't do that!*

I had to think quickly, as the next words out of my mouth would likely frame where this conversation was going. I knew that I didn't have an immediate solution for this very obvious problem. I was two months behind in my house payment and had no immediate resource to fix it. What to say?

"David, are you sure my payment hasn't been misapplied?" *Genius!* I thought. *Misdirection, if nothing else, will buy me time. Wonder if he'll buy this?*

"Chuck, I don't think so," replied David. "But let me check some things and get back to you right after lunch."

"David, that'll be great, and I'll check on my end as well, but I'm confident the payments have been made."

That conversation ended, but another was just about to begin. You see, I still had a problem. David would find nothing other than the clear fact that he was right. Those two payments had not been made. The only thing that I'd successfully done was delay the inevitable. Without a doubt, I had to find a solution to my problem quickly or man up and admit that I was overextended and underfunded. I had too much debt.

At that time, I happened to be designated as a trustee for an education trust for one of my clients. He had set money aside so it could grow tax deferred for his children's college educations. The kick was, the person who established the trust could not be the trustee. My client had to pick someone he trusted to manage his children's education funds. I was the trusted one and had been placed in the powerful position of managing these funds for his two young children.

It was a Friday afternoon when I received David's unexpected call. The other partners in the office were gone. They had business they were working on, and so I sat there alone, thinking to myself, *Oh crap, what am I going to do?* I couldn't get my partners' help. Sure was a bad time for them to be gone. My mother lived in Baltimore, and in those days, it wasn't so easy to effect an electronic transfer of funds…so that wasn't an option either.

It's funny – perhaps the better word is *odd* – how, when faced with a significant challenge, we begin to have an internal dialogue seeking a solution. Now, so many years later, I've had the privilege of talking with many folks who at one point in their lives, made a significant choice that began with an internal dialogue much like mine. Mind you now, not all inner dialogues are bad, but I have to wonder if we might be wise to pay attention to those discussions we have with ourselves, as it seems many of them result in life choices that can't be undone.

Buck used to say, "A negative mind will never give you a positive life." Man, was he right!

To solve my problem back then, I had to make a decision. I had the chance right then and there to make a positive choice, but my mind was so wrapped up with negative thinking that I was already headed in the wrong direction. Negative thinking is disempowering. I wish I had known then what I know now. Not to say that I don't still have negative thoughts from time to time. I do. But I'm also aware of what that negative talk sounds like and feels like, and I recognize what the consequences can be. It never leads to anywhere positive.

• • •

I had to make a decision. I had the chance right then and there to make a positive choice, but my mind was so wrapped up with negative thinking that I was already headed in the wrong direction. Negative thinking is disempowering.

• • •

After David's call, I began a dialogue in my head, which was quite normal for me. I chatted with myself often –

perhaps the natural side of a Gemini (if you follow astrology – I don't). As a side note: In 1987, if you were driving down the road talking to yourself, people might look at you and think you were crazy. I mean, most people don't just talk to themselves out loud. Today, if you're driving down the road talking, people will just think you're on a Bluetooth, which raises the question: How many crazy people are driving around talking to themselves?!

Back to that day. Stop for a minute and answer this question: What do you think you would do in my situation?

Although I had deflected blame and made a wrong choice by lying, I had bought time, but only about two hours. I could have come clean and told my partners I needed a few thousand dollars. That would have been the best bet, but I had to maintain the illusion that I was financially solvent, and they were not physically available to help me right then. Partners were out. That wasn't a solution.

Option two was that I could call my mother and say, "Hey, Mom, I need to borrow a little bit of money and I'll pay you back in a couple of months." That would have been easy, except there was no time. Even if she were willing to cut a check and send it to me, it would take a few days, arriving via snail mail. Then I'd have to deposit it in the bank before turning around to pay the banker. That just wasn't going to solve my problem in the two-hour window I had.

The last honest option was to go to the bank and say I needed a loan, but that would put a spotlight on my own inability to manage money, which just wasn't an option I was willing to consider.

My first significant foray into the world of unethical choices began with a dialogue that went something like this:

"Chuck in Trouble" said, *I need a quick source of funds to pay my house payment before I get in trouble with David at the bank.*

"Trustee Chuck," sensing an opportunity, responded, *While this is highly unconventional, I could advance some funds from the trust.* Trustee Chuck knew he had the duty to get the best return on the client's investment (perfect rationalization for an unethical choice), and so an advance with a ten percent interest return guaranteed by Chuck in Trouble's tax season bonus would be a windfall to the trust.

Chuck in Trouble, sensing a quick solution, promised to pay ten percent interest on the two thousand that would be advanced (stolen – let's call it what it really was) from the trust. *I will pay back $2,200 and do it by the end of April.*

Well, now, ten percent paid in a quarter – that was really a forty percent return, which was a great return for the client's money and with very little risk because, as the thief and trustee, I knew I was going to get the bonus. *After all,* I thought in my head, *this is really just a short-term problem, and here's a short-term solution.*

There I was, having this conversation between two people. One is me with a conservative hat on (looking like a banker from Monopoly) talking to my desperate self about how I'm going to take money from a trust to solve the problem that, by the way, nobody knows about but me. I had a serious need, and it wasn't really the money itself. That was just the tip of the iceberg.

I had a *need* – on the surface it appeared to be just money.

To solve that need I had *opportunity* – the college trust fund.

However, to make the whole thing work (in my head, I mean), I had to find a way to make theft okay. That component is called *rationalization*.

The rationalization was that I was going to pay it back. I'm not a thief. I'm just an opportunistic borrower from a private lending source. It's really just a loan. No harm, no foul – so to speak. Rationalization is what allowed me to sleep at night knowing I was willingly in the throes of stealing money.

As expected, the second call did come, and David said with more concern in his voice, "Chuck, we've looked at our records...."

Before he could finish the sentence, I blurted, "David, I'm so embarrassed. You don't need to go any further. You're absolutely right. I did not make the house payment. I cannot believe this has slipped through the cracks. This is so highly embarrassing to me. You know, we just had our first son, Rob, at the end of November and, well, my wife pays the bills." This too was not true, but to make the excuse plausible, it made sense that I needed to expand the story a bit.

Notice something and think not only about my story, but others I know you're thinking about right now. See how easy it is, once you step on that slippery slope, to take one step right after the other into the world of lying and deceit. First I convinced myself that theft was a loan, and now I was openly lying to a member of my Sunday school class. How quickly "Thou shalt not lie" was forgotten.

"I thought she was taking care of the bills, and she thought I was handling them. It never crossed my mind she wasn't, and so here we are. I'm so sorry. I'll bring you a check in an hour." Seems like I was playing Adam and Eve all over again. I had to blame somebody, so I gave the blame to my wife.

David said, "Listen, let me tell you something…." And then he began to talk lowly into the phone, "I passed a bad check once when I was in college. We all have these things."

Wow! We had this male bonding moment. I was behind on my house payment, but it wasn't intentional, at least as far as David knew. He had passed a bad check once, but it wasn't intentional, at least as far as I knew. So the best of us can make stupid choices or mistakes and, as long as we fix it, we're okay. That was the message, and with it, I admit, came a sigh of relief.

Now the pressure was off, and I did exactly what I said, except the reality was that I stole the money to pay the house payment. And in order to sleep at night, I created the illusion that I was really borrowing money. Funny thing is, I did sit down at the computer with the word processing program and typed up a promissory note, which was frankly worthless. It kept up the illusion and supported the rationalization. Keep in mind, I'm the only person responsible for the activity on this trust, so no one was really going to see it. But to make it "legitimate" (at least in my head) I typed up a note: *With sound mind and body, I do hereby blah, blah, blah.* With the note finished, I went down to the bank and made the house payment. David and I had a nice little laugh about it. Everything was fine – or so it seemed.

A series of choices led up to that pivotal decision. But what were those series of choices, exactly? Is it possible that in some form or fashion, all our choices lead us to life-changing moments? I suppose I could go all the way back to when I was first capable of choosing. Choices like cheating on a test or telling someone a lie because I didn't want to deal with the consequences of telling them the truth. Multitudes of little choices with no seeming consequence just got bigger and bigger until the day the ultimate consequence arrived, and I stepped foot into federal prison.

Tyler, a friend from my college days, shared with me not long ago about the experience his son had with credit cards. Of course, financial institutions target market young folks like crazy. They have no real credit history so they haven't yet developed a bad credit score. And, well, what better way to get someone hooked on consuming than to give him or her access to easy money?

Seems his son Ray got his first credit solicitation when he was a freshman in college. Like most kids, Ray quickly maxed out his credit line, and not wanting his dad to think he was incapable of handling his affairs, he responded to another card offer accessing more credit from another provider. Ray used some of his new credit to make a few payments on his first card. Alas, the temptation to have more new things was a bit overwhelming, and Ray quickly had both cards maxed out. Ray knew he shouldn't do it, but the temptation of having it right now was just too great.

Reality is that often we get a new credit card and make those small purchases, paying it off in a month. It's not until about the third or fourth month that we start paying just the minimum. You charge a little bit, pay it off, charge a little bit, pay it off, and you feel good about it. And then you find the bigger purchases, and you think, *Well, I can pay this off in a couple months,* and the next thing you know, you have a growing balance on your credit card and can only afford the minimum payments, which means that in thirty-five years you'll finally pay off the appliance you bought that has long since become obsolete.

The choices we make tend to compound. In my case, I made a lot of little choices that took me to a place where I was incapable of effectively managing my financial affairs. To make matters worse, I shared that secret with no one. Since my wife had no clue, she made no effort to adjust her spending habits, and I made no effort to stop her. Between the two of us, we lived a lifestyle that was beyond our means.

Day in and day out, those small, insignificant choices compounded. Compounded choices can lead to a complex solution, and for my wife and me the outcome was catastrophic change – change that neither of us wanted and, odd as it may sound, neither of us expected.

The truth is that once we begin to make unethical choices, even if only a little bit, over time it can become a habit! My time in prison seared that into my conscious knowing. Every choice has a consequence. It stands to reason, then, that if bad choices earned me prison, then equally good, ethical choices should create a better outcome. Now it was time to test that theory. I was sure hoping it would work!

Chapter 4

IS IT REALLY DIFFERENT TODAY?

ARE THINGS REALLY THAT MUCH DIFFERENT TODAY? Do we seem to make better, more ethical choices? Truth be told, at least from my perspective, I don't think so. Most people don't have savings put away that would cover six months of their life should they experience a catastrophic event. A good number of people today live month to month, and in some cases, credit card to credit card. So long as everything seems to be okay, and their cards are active, life is in balance – or so it seems. But all is not always as it seems.

What happens when life gets out of balance? What happens when the economy changes? What happens when you lose a job? What happens when you discover that the banking system, which encouraged you to borrow money against your house, now calls in your adjustable-rate mortgage? What happens when you owe more than your house is worth? What happens when you lose your health? What happens when life dramatically changes?

I had moved from socially acceptable to unethical actions, and then to frankly illegal actions. It's a slippery slope and one that, if you're not careful, you can quickly lose your footing on. I had been on that slope, but this was the first time I put my skis on and said, "Let's ride down the mountain!"

At the end of tax season, I paid back the money I stole with interest. Does that make it right? Heavens no! All it meant was that, in my head, I had confirmed that my unethical, illegal action was in fact okay. I successfully rationalized my illegal behavior. Paying back what I had stolen cemented the idea that it was really just a loan and I had done nothing wrong.

"I mean, seriously, if you steal money from someone and pay it back with interest, then it can't be theft. Right?" That's what I said to myself over and over. At some point your mind can eventually play tricks on you. A fully rationalizing mind can be so clever. It fools you into believing that what it's saying isn't horse crap... it's chocolate! After all, it's brown, isn't it?

It didn't take me long to realize that this newfound source of money (my own private lending source, so to speak) was easy to access. My unethical, illegal choice seemed to yield no consequence. That word *consequence* is key in determining the probability of whether a person will voluntarily choose, whether personally or professionally, to act unethically. The easiest place to see this is with youth. A kid (tween or teen) will often take the course of least resistance in order to solve a problem. For example, they

• • •

"I mean, seriously, if you steal money from someone and pay it back with interest, then it can't be theft. Right?"

• • •

may cheat on a test they're ill-prepared to take if they feel they can get away with it. Once they succeed without any known consequence, the unethical action will, in many cases, become their preferred method of dealing with the issue or others like it. *After all,* they rationalize, *what my teachers (or parents) don't know won't hurt me.* Make no mistake – this is also true in business.

This idea of performing unethical actions without consequences reminds me of the old philosophical question: If a tree falls in the woods and no one is there to hear it, does it make a sound? As the argument goes, since no one is there to hear it fall, we don't know if there's a sound or not. Of course, we know there's a sound! But since no person ever hears it, that information never makes it into human consciousness. That same idea can be carried over into how we rationalize our actions when we do something that's wrong or unethical, and there's no immediate consequence. Does it mean there actually is no consequence? Or does it mean we simply haven't perceived one? Little choices we make can reinforce the concept that we can get away with things in life without any consequences...that is, until there really is one.

This simple concept, in many ways, reveals the seeds of corruption. In politics, for example, once people get away with dishonesty, it becomes okay, even politically acceptable. Even those of us who aren't active in politics start to believe that, since everybody does it, it must be all right. We believe that every politician gets a little bribe here or there. It's become the norm. Of course, it's rarely just a little thing. The corruption starts off small, and then grows bigger.

The same pattern of corruption holds for business. You start out with a small fib, an exaggeration or a misrepresentation. Then, all of a sudden, you begin to believe it's just the way to do business, no matter that it's illegal, unethical, or whatever label you want to use. It continues because you got away with it once, you got away with it twice, and over time you and those around you no longer perceive it as a bad thing. This slippery slope of unethical conduct can happen in our personal lives, too. Even when teaching children how to behave, if you let them get away with unacceptable behavior the first few times, you're going to have a hard time changing that behavior later in life.

I was being interviewed on a radio show recently, and in today's environment, that's often done via phone or Skype. The female interviewer (I won't mention her name as it's recognizable) was obviously at home when the interview was being conducted. In the middle of the interview, in the background, I could hear the faint ring of a phone and knew it wasn't mine. Now if I could hear it faintly, then I assume it was loud and distracting for her. But what happened next created quite the talking point for future presentations.

Moments later, the ringing ended. I assumed that the caller had hung up. Seems that wasn't the case. Next I hear the interviewer's daughter – from the sound of her voice, she must have been four or five years old – barging into the room, talking with excitement to her mother.

"Mommy, Aunt Sally wants to speak to you," she said with the cutest little voice.

"Tell her I'm in the shower," my interviewer quickly instructed her daughter as she got back to the interview, telling me that she could edit this portion out.

"Hmm," I thought. "There's a lesson here!"

Instead of telling the truth, which would have been easy, my interviewer elected, unconsciously perhaps, to teach her daughter to lie when the truth might be perceived as inconvenient. So we start teaching our kids at a young age to lie, and by the time kids become teens, when we try to put our foot down, it's way too late because they've already formed in their mind what's right and wrong.

Over the course of my own life, I made many small choices that led me to a major turning point. On that day, when I received the phone call about my delinquent house payments, I crossed the line and did something unethical and illegal. I had a need and did whatever I had to in order to meet it. I had been conditioned and accustomed to lying, and it was surprisingly easy to take that lie to that next level.

For me, the need that was great enough to allow me to be dishonest was money. Others may have different needs, which can lead to other choices that finally cross the ethical line.

On day two in prison, Buck asked me, "What you in here for?"

Since these were the very first words he spoke to me, I thought for a moment. I had to be tough (or so I thought – guess I had watched too many prison movies), so I mustered up my toughest self with a posture like John Wayne and a swagger like Clint Eastwood and uttered, "I'm a liar and a thief."

"Word?"

"Word?" I replied to Buck, having no clue what he was saying.

"Yeah, word?"

Buck's one-word question fell on deaf ears. I had no clue what he was saying or, worse yet, how to reply.

"You don't know what I'm talking about, does ya?" With that oddly uttered question, Buck left the cell in frustration.

How did I land in prison? The first step had no consequence. The second step was easy. I discovered I could do this. I came to believe it was acceptable because all I was doing was just borrowing from a private source of ready cash. I did it again and paid it back again, until one day I had become nothing more than a liar and a thief.

Buck came back to the cell almost as rapidly as he'd left. "Yo, man. I'll makes you a deal!"

Make me a deal, I thought. *I've been here twenty-four hours and a convict's wanting to make me a deal.* Then it hit me. *I'm a convict, too. Okay, I'm listening.*

"You won't survive in here. You don't know the lingo or how to act," Buck shared with animation. "I'll teach you the lingo and how to act. I'll even have your back! If you'll teach me how to speak correctly, so when I get out I'll have a chance at getting a real job."

Buck's last request landed hard on me, as I saw us both needing to find our second chance – a fresh start at life that included making ethical, empowering choices, not choices based on short-term, ill-gotten solutions to temporary life imbalances. Buck showed his humanity to me and gave me a deeper reason to make this experience one that could have value. If every choice has a consequence, I may not know immediately the positive consequence that would come from prison, but I had to believe that one was possible. Buck opened the door to the possibility of something greater.

I didn't enjoy prison, but Buck kept his word. He taught me how to survive while there, and I taught him how to speak without Ebonics so he would hopefully get a "real" job when he got out. Buck and I became fast friends. Among the many things he taught me was that you can find people with integrity anywhere you are. Buck was a clear example of that. He acted ethically in even the vilest of places.

I'll never forget one day, when Buck and I were cleaning our cell, out of the clear blue he asked, "Have you ever been bitten by an elephant?" Now that was the darndest question I had ever heard someone ask. I thought: *What would make someone ask such a dumb question?*

With a piercing glance, I answered, "No! Now that's one hell of a question."

Buck had one of those mischievous grins on his face, one he was desperately trying to hide, the kind that I'd see when I knew something else was coming my way. "What about a mosquito? Ever been bitten by a mosquito?"

And then he said, "It's the little things in life that'll bite you!"

He was right. He was right whether you related it to choices from my past or from his own, or whether you apply it to the life we live today. Most people – I mean ninety-nine percent – don't wake up one day and say, "I'm

• • •

*You can find people with
integrity anywhere you are.
Buck was a clear example of
that. He acted ethically in
even the vilest of places.*

• • •

going to do something today that will change my life for the worst." Or for the best. It just doesn't happen that way. It's the little choices with no apparent consequence that lull us into the belief that, if there's no immediate consequence, then there will never be any consequence.

With me, it started as a little thing. Truth be known, there were probably other, even smaller things I'd chosen over the course of my life that allowed me to think that stealing (called *borrowing* in my head) would be an acceptable choice to solve the problem of a delinquent house payment. That's what Buck meant when he said, "It's the little things in life that will bite you."

I learned firsthand that every choice has a consequence. Prison was not fun. The idea was that punishment and being stripped naked, both literally and figuratively, would have the effect of breaking down your ego barrier and reducing you to the core of your existence. I had to accept that the choices I made got me there. But there was a question I kept asking over and over while behind those prison walls: If my bad choices got me here, is it possible that good choices, once I was released, could be the foundation for redemption?

Chapter 5

BUCK AND CHUCK AND THE POWER OF NEED!

I'D NEVER KNOWN A DRUG DEALER – actually never thought about it or wanted to. But Buck was an enigma to me. I suppose it's easy to see someone else's flaws. It's much harder, however, to see your own, since we look out of the rosy-tinted glasses of our own mental perception. I had so many questions for my young cellmate.

"Buck, tell me the truth." I always thought that phrase was funny because it infers that most people would rather tell you a lie. Perhaps that's true. "Why did you start selling drugs in the first place? I mean, didn't you know you'd get caught?"

"I'll tell you if you'll tell me," Buck replied with a semi-grin that made me wonder if he was making fun of me.

Buck's response caught me a bit off guard. Yet, as it seemed to go with us, he would quickly turn my question around to help me see beyond my illusions. Buck was good like that, and I found during my time with him that I learned far more than I ever would in a psychology class. Buck had no formal training, but he was naturally talented when it came to seeing through people's illusions and boring straight into the truth of a situation. Buck's the kind of guy you'd like to mastermind with, a person who will tell you the truth when you need to hear it but don't want to. And he'd do so with a heart of love.

"Deal," I replied.

"When I was thirteen, I began to notice that some brothers seemed to want for nothing. They had money, and with that they had things...and girls too. Then there were others who worked after school – mostly at fast food joints – or helping their mom do janitorial work. They were okay but just didn't have the bling that the other brothers had. I wanted what they had!"

One thing I learned with Buck, he didn't hold back. He spoke his mind. That was something I had to come to grips with. Honestly, I can't recall anyone who was as straightforward as Buck, and not in a bad way. His candor seemed to cut through the illusions that many of us wanted to share and went straight to the core of real truth. And, frankly, most of the time Buck was spot-on.

Buck went on with his story. "One of my homeboys told me one day as I was approaching my fourteenth birthday that he'd cut me in on some of the action if I'd take some of his stash over to a homeboy across town. For that he gave me the equivalent of three days' pay for the homies at the fast food joints. Chuck, that was the easiest money I ever made. Ya see, I needs what I wants."

• • •

Funny how we confuse
needs *with* wants.

• • •

Buck's last comment – I need what I want – hit me like a ton of bricks. Looking back, I felt the same way. Funny how we learn to confuse *needs* with *wants*. Perhaps that's innate, natural behavior in humans. Or maybe we learn it somewhere along the way. I don't know. What I do know is that we're programmed at a young age to confuse the two so that when we become young adults, we often can't effectively define the difference between the two.

Needs and wants are powerful motivators of behavior. We're taught in so many ways that we need to be like others. In fact, advertisers use this aspect of human behavior often, sending subliminal suggestions that "many people prefer." They know that deep inside, we have a need to be like others. "Many people prefer" is nothing more than hypnotic, suggestive language that quickly goes to one's core, strongly influencing opinion and behavior.

Have you ever wondered when smoking became popular in the U.S.? During World War II, cigarette companies provided cigarettes to the military at minimal cost for guys in combat. "Why?" you might ask. Partly it was because cigarettes are laced with nicotine, which supposedly gives you a rush. Such a rush is helpful in combat. It's also pleasurable and addictive. A multibillion-dollar industry recognized that if they hooked you on becoming a cigarette smoker – partly because the products were highly addictive and partly because they were building a culture where everybody did it – they were creating customers for life. Of course, smoking might possibly shorten your lifespan and harm your health. This was a slippery slope for many who couldn't quit when they wanted to.

The cigarette companies created a perceived need. Now, we all know that no one needs to smoke a cigarette. People can be influenced to choose to smoke for various reasons, but smoking is not a need. Yet it's common to hear people say, "I need a cigarette." Funny how a want becomes a need, especially when the behavior is addictive. Make no mistake – it isn't just drugs that can be addictive. Money, gambling, sex, and many other things can be just as addictive as smoking.

Think about it. At the top of the slippery slope, smoking was cool and everybody did it. At the bottom was an inability to quit. Teens who picked up the smoking habit did it because they saw how cool it was in the movies. After all, James Dean looked mighty tough with the cigarette dangling from his lips. None of them ever sat back and considered how cigarettes were laced with drugs they were unable to give up. They didn't think about the high cost of paying for them – with their money, their time, their health, and possibly their lives. Cigarettes made tobacco companies billions upon billions of dollars. Something that was once a want became an inescapable need.

Likewise, kids away from home for the first time at college typically get all kinds of invitations for their first credit card, which is very enticing. So they sign up for it. It's so easy. Then they charge for the first time, a second time, and by the middle of the semester, the credit card is charged up and they hope the parents will pay for it. Or they quickly find that they're offered new cards with balance transfer options, giving them a way to fix their problem and satisfy their perceived need for more stuff.

As the credit card offers continue to pour in, borrowers develop a credit history. They establish the beginnings of a Ponzi-like scheme, moving their balances from one card to the other, depending on who's offering the lowest interest rates. At one time, balance transfer rates were zero with no transfer fees. Those golden days are over, but not before the borrowers had racked up tremendous amounts of debt.

The idea of need is so often generated by our surroundings and societal expectations. Most everyone reading this book has heard the phrase "keeping up with the Joneses." We might laugh and say, "Well, that's not me." But, in reality, multiple studies provide consistent results showing that the behavior of one person in a group can influence the behavior of many.

At Christmas, most of us are conditioned to buy gifts for each other, and if someone gives a gift to us, we feel obligated to give back. In fact, the entire Christmas season seems to start earlier and earlier for retailers every year. They know that we're conditioned to respond to feelings of generosity during the Christmas holiday. So, what was once a shopping season in the U.S. that started at Thanksgiving and extended to Christmas Day now begins in October, before Halloween.

Christmas giving for many is simple; you want to give to all your family members, extended family, and close friends. Next thing you know, people in the neighborhood are giving something as well, and you're forced to ask yourself how much you're really going to spend this Christmas. The vast majority of retailers in the U.S. depend upon holiday sales to make them profitable. Actually, the economy pretty much relies on this established pattern.

It's amazing what happens when you try to break ingrained patterns such as Christmas giving. In recent years, my wife and I decided that this Christmas-giving stuff was for the birds. We recognized that when we needed something or wanted something, we generally bought it right then. We didn't wait. And at Christmas, we and our kids and our parents would buy something because we thought we had to. We often faced the dilemma of keeping a gift so as not to hurt the gift giver's feelings or returning the gift for something we actually liked. We came upon a solution: "In the spirit of giving, let's elect not to give to each other and, rather, give to those less fortunate – those truly in need." Some of the kids got into that idea, but some didn't. And our parents, now in their late seventies and early eighties, were very much opposed.

Apple would like you to believe that you need one of their watches, and they do a very persuasive job of helping you believe that too. You could buy just the basic model, but Apple encourages you to want more. You don't need the $10,000 watch either, but Apple positions it well. Ten thousand bucks on the top end means you're the one with the coolest technology anywhere. But Apple knows that you're most likely to go for the watch positioned in the middle – the $500-ish watch. The real question to millions of consumers is: Do you really *need* an Apple Watch or do you just *want* an Apple Watch? Apple would eventually like to turn your want into a need. When that happens, watch (no pun intended) what happens to Apple stock and consumer behavior.

Recently I saw Anthony Robbins being interviewed. He was asked an interesting question: "What is the last thing you purchased?" His answer: "A jet."

That was a bit unexpected, I thought. I don't think in my wildest dreams I'd answer that question with "I went and bought a jet."

Obviously, Mr. Robbins felt like he needed it. Why? Well, if he's like me, he might have had this conversation with himself: *I'm Anthony Robbins. I'm in high demand; and so it's far more convenient, comfortable, and efficient for me to go to the airport, hop in my private jet, and be on my way. Far better than having to wait in lines and try to fit on a regular plane.*

• • •

Once you interpret something as a need, you take action to get it. That's human nature.

• • •

Anthony Robbins' needs are different than Chuck Gallagher's needs. And Chuck's needs are different than the needs of somebody who lives in the projects in Ferguson, Missouri. Everyone has a different set of needs. So the question becomes not "What is the need?" as much as "What do we perceive the need to be?" and "What are we doing to create those needs?"

For many of us, our initial programming as a child creates the foundation for our future behavior. Raised by a single parent (my dad died when I was two), I look back at my childhood and feel it was good. We weren't wealthy, but we always had food. My mother was a lovely lady, always wanting the best for me. What she taught me about money was the concept of leverage. We grew up on credit. In the small mill village in North Carolina, common practice was to have merchant accounts with consumers. For example, if you got sick and went to the doctor, you'd put your balance on an account and make payments to clear the balance. The same was true for medications purchased at the local pharmacy. "Put it on my account," my mother would say, and with that we would leave with prescription in hand.

Money was tight, so by the time I was in high school, we lived in a housing project. At the time, housing projects didn't have quite the same stigma as they do today, but fundamentally we were living in the projects. In those days, you washed your clothes and hung them out to dry. Today you don't do that. I rarely see clotheslines being used anymore. Today people need a dryer. They don't actually need it; they want it. The clothesline works just fine. But we've become conditioned to believe that as we move up the ladder, or whatever ascending metaphor you want to use, our needs change. Whether your need is basic shelter or moving out of homelessness, or whether you're Anthony Robbins who feels like he needs his own private jet, it's perceived as a legitimate, got-to-be-fulfilled need. Once something is interpreted as a need, you must take action to get it.

Let me repeat this truth. Once you interpret something as a need, you take action to get it. That's human nature.

It's important to balance the difference between needs and wants. Parents and children talk about this and negotiate it all the time. Most parents will attest that teaching a child how something is a want and not a need is often a fruitless lesson. Telling your teenage daughter that a new phone is a want and not a need leaves her looking at you like you're a two-headed monster. Why? Because emotionally she feels like it's a frickin' need! So you can talk about it intellectually all day long, but the question is: Does it make any difference? Perhaps the more accurate way to differentiate a need from a want is to determine the level of emotion you attach to the desire and what you're willing to do about it.

For example, there are those who find comfort food to be the cure for anxiety or the emptiness they feel inside, which is not physical hunger but something deeper – a painful hole. Comfort food satisfies (or at least people think it does) an emotional need. Because a long-term solution to filling the hole is difficult, or even unknown, they instead turn to the short-term full feeling that comes from food. Do they need the food? No. Do they want the food? Yes. But they'll tell you they need it because emotionally, there's something missing from their lives, and they're compelled to fill it. Intellectually we can easily define the difference between a need and a want, but in the end, the action of fulfilling a need is based not on intellect, but on emotion.

About a month into my incarceration, Buck asked me a more direct question, one that required me to really think: "Chuck, you stole money. What made you think you needed to do that?"

Buck's question was simple, yet it was also deep. Now, I could have given him a shallow answer like, "I needed to pay my mortgage." But that would only be half true. Yes, I needed to pay my delinquent mortgage, but the reality was I had a deeper need. Just like with comfort food, my comfort was feeding a need with things.

In the midst of my predicament, I quickly discovered that I had access to a private stash of money readily available to fulfill my every need or misidentified perceived need. As if the trust fund were a credit card, I began with the certainty I would pay back whatever I took in a timely manner, and all would be honest. I used money from the trust fund for my house payment. Then I tapped into it again to expand my growing needs arising out of the better life I was earning, deserving, and emotionally certain I needed. These expenses included clothes, cars, watches, shoes, etc. Expanding my lifestyle externally created the illusion of success, and I so deeply wanted success – something I perceived I hadn't had as a child.

Quickly, with my ill-gotten funding source, I had a BMW. Six months later I traded it for a Mercedes. Six months later I traded the Mercedes for a Porsche. Then I went back to a BMW, only to decide I really needed a Jaguar. If you're buying a car every six months, you're losing money. You'd think that a CPA would know better, but when you're in the midst of making choices that come from a deep unfilled emotional hole, no amount of reason will easily change your choices.

I shared with Buck the truth…the whole truth.

"Buck, the truth is my behavior went back a long way. I didn't start out being a liar and deceiver, but I have to be honest. It started when I first connected with my wife when we were dating in high school." Talking with Buck and looking back was a strange experience, as it hit me that how I interacted with the girl who would become my wife showed what some would call a character flaw. An area of my life needed attention and healing. But, of course, I had no clue about that at the time. My subconscious thoughts brought that need to the surface; I was just too blind to know what was going on.

"What are you talking about?" Buck asked with a strange look on his face. Sometimes it took Buck and me a minute or two (or three) to get on the same page. We came from different worlds, and to get our communication in sync could be a challenge.

"Look, I met my wife in high school. I'll never forget that, when I called her for our first date, she turned me down. She honestly had no interest in me. I didn't know it at the time but, being nice, she suggested a rain check. I was thrilled. I was like the dude in the movie *Dumb and Dumber.* When he asks the girl, 'Is there a chance?' and she says, having no interest at all in him, 'One in a million.'

He replies with enthusiasm, 'So there's a chance!' Well, I was just like Jim Carrey in the movie – a freaking eternal optimist. So she gave me the rain check, and I was thrilled!"

Buck rolled back in his bunk laughing. To a black boy from the hood, a needy white boy being thrilled at a rain check was foreign. Fortunately for me, instead of being judgmental, Buck was understanding. "So what does this have to do with you stealing money?"

"Look," I replied. "She was a league above me, the kind of girl who was a cheerleader in junior high and dates the quarterback who drives a sports car. She was a cool person. And I was an average person to her, at best. Heck, I lived in the projects.

"So what I did in that relationship is I bought her love. I wasn't a cool kid in high school, so I had to compensate somehow. Or at least that's how I saw it then. So what did I do? I bought her records – they were vinyl records at the time. Or a tape for her car. Sometimes, I'd slip off school grounds, which was against the rules, to buy her lunch and bring it back to put in her locker. All of her friends were swooning about what this guy was doing for her. The whole premise of our relationship was based on the idea that I would do whatever it took, including something illegal, to show her how much I loved her."

"Man, you were whooped," Buck said with a huge laugh. "You can't let women get you that bad. Damn, man!"

Buck was right, but then again he and I came from different worlds. To me it was no big deal at the time. Only later would I see it as the slippery slope it was. I started a pattern of behavior that got worse over time. I wanted her, so I was willing to do what other people were unwilling to do. Since I wasn't the quarterback, I did what was in my power to persuade her. She didn't ask; I just did it. But I set up the pattern of behavior that I would do whatever it took to meet the perceived need, and she developed the pattern of expecting that I would do whatever she wanted.

Then there was the added support that I was doing the right thing – winning her affection – by breaking the rules. Everyone, all our friends, knew I was breaking the rules to meet her needs or take care of her, and their reaction was positive. They said things like, "Wow, look what he's doing!" From her parents to her friends, there was clear social reinforcement for my actions. The only person opposed to my actions was my mother, and she was the one person I refused to listen to. Hmm...how often do I hear that today from disgruntled parents?

"So, did you get caught?" Buck asked with a smirk on his face. He was finding this conversation humorous. I sounded like such a wimp to him, yet he knew deep down that what I was telling him is what landed me in prison. We both knew that something that starts simple can have profound consequences. We knew that because we were both living proof of it.

"There was a consequence, but it wasn't significant. I spent time in detention for about six weeks until my junior year was over and was told, 'You know better!' It was about

• • •

The closer people are to something, such as a wrong choice, the harder it is to determine that it's taking place.

• • •

as serious as a slap on the wrist. I got punished, but that added to my street cred, showing that I really 'loved' her. The experience of high school and its consequence just wasn't significant enough for me to stop the behavior, and the cycle repeated itself until the consequence became much more serious than detention.

"Buck, looking back on it, I think the behavior also didn't stop because I was just too close to the situation to see the problem."

"Yeah, I get that. Seen that too much with my homies in the hood." Buck quickly moved from finding humor to finding truth – a truth he could understand.

The closer people are to something, such as a wrong choice, the harder it is to determine that it's taking place. If you're standing at the foot of the trees in the forest, you can't tell which is the tallest tree. There's a perspective you have looking up that doesn't allow you to see what the real top looks like. So you can't pick out the tallest tree in a dense forest. On the other hand, if you're in a plane or helicopter and are flying over, you can easily identify the tallest tree. So sometimes, to be able to see something taking place, you need to find a different perspective.

"Being with my girlfriend made me cool, accepted. You know what I mean, Buck?"

"Yeah, guess we all seek to be accepted somehow. My way was dealin'. Look what that got me!"

"Well, for me, that need I was walking around with was built into my marriage from the beginning of our relationship. Guess it was destined to fail," I said with deep sadness. I found it easy to carry the weight of the failure of my marriage on my shoulders. *If I'd been better, stronger, maybe it would have worked,* I often thought.

Some might say it should have been obvious to anyone that there was something weird here, but I'm sure my wife never caught on. While she may disagree, I believe she was complicit in creating the problem, even if she wasn't involved in the crime. I think she was too close to really get what was going on, and she had her own needs and wants too. I set up the pattern, and she easily complied. For example, she would purchase whatever she wanted, mostly stuff for the house, and then having grown accustomed to money always being available, she would tell me what she bought and say that I needed to put money in the account. As long as there was never a "no," it meant there was always a "yes."

A stronger man would have told her "no." But then a stronger man wouldn't have set up the pattern in the first place. Looking back, I should have told her no, but buried in this charade was one of the most profound needs of all – I didn't want to be rejected. So there was an emotional need that said to me, "Well, if you want to maintain her love, then this is what you do. You always provide, regardless of what it takes."

My need was the old adage, "Happy wife, happy life." I met that need over and over again. I needed for there to be peace and acceptance. I needed for her to be happy with me. These are basic human needs – to feel a sense of belonging, to be accepted. Those are real needs, not wants. Yet, the question looms: How does one go about meeting those needs? Not everyone turns to unethical behavior to meet them.

"When the grand illusion I created collapsed, several things took place, Buck," I continued. We were deep into a conversation that was going to create the foundation for much deeper discussions to follow, although I didn't know this at the time. "First, it was devastating to my wife. She was faced with the huge concern of *What will people think?* If her perception and reality weren't matching, it was earth-shattering to her. She dreaded the judgment that she thought would take her from upper-middle class or higher and throw her down, possibly to the projects where I started out. Emotionally, that was devastating for

• • •

*Is it easy to open doors
that have been hidden
and sheltered? No. But
it's incredibly valuable.*

• • •

her. For me, however, it was freeing because I was finally out of this vicious cycle I'd been living in."

"So you felt good in a way?"

"No, Buck. None of this felt good. Honestly, I felt like shit for what I'd done to my wife, my partners and my family. I didn't know what to do or where to turn. But I did know that at least the cat was out of the bag, and something different had to be done. It all started with a simple pattern I created."

Patterns can be incredibly important in our lives and choices. Patterns create the foundation for the lives we live and the choices we make. And all too often, our patterns are loaded at such an early age that we have no conscious awareness that they even exist.

As an example, I have a dear friend in her early sixties who's extremely obese. We've talked about it, and she can clearly see her pattern and the reason why she can't lose weight. Why? Very simple! She was sexually abused as a child. It was a horrendous experience, and she learned that if she created an obese body, a less than desirable body, she would be unappealing and could therefore protect herself from physical abuse. This pattern of behavior became a need to her – one of protection. Did she need excess food? No! But it became a mechanism to provide the weight, and the weight was a perceived need to provide the protection she felt she had to have.

When we have a perceived need, whether it's actually a need or a want doesn't really make a difference. In the mind, in the emotion, it's a need, the fulfillment of which creates an outcome that has consequences. My need wasn't the money for the house payment. Not really. That was the surface issue fundamentally created by a far, far deeper need and pattern that was set much earlier in my life.

The foundation for our choices – whether it's what we eat for lunch or deeper choices, such as whom we select as a spouse – is based on our need or perceived need. As we end this chapter, ask yourself a few questions: (1) What was the last major decision you made and what need did it satisfy? (2) Think of a time when you made a terrible choice. Now, looking back on it, what need were you trying to meet? (3) Recall a time from your childhood when you lied to your parent(s). What caused you to lie? What did you think the lie would help you accomplish or avoid?

You can begin to answer these questions if you're willing to open some doors into your own programming, much as I've had to open those doors for myself. Is it easy to open doors that have been hidden and sheltered? No. But it's incredibly valuable.

Chapter 6

WHEN OPPORTUNITY KNOCKS

"You ever thought about just how easy it is for folks to stray off the straight and narrow?" Buck's question, like so many he would ask over our time together in prison, would be the catalyst for more than one night's discussion. "I wanted to be cool and have money just like the street punks I looked up to. Now I'm in prison just like the rest of them. Shoulda seen that coming," Buck said with a rather exasperated look on his face.

"Yeah, Buck, I've thought about it a lot. Never in my wildest dreams would anyone, especially me, think that I'd become an inmate in federal prison." With a bit of a grin on my face, and remembering my high school yearbook,

I said, "Most likely to be a convicted felon." That's not a picture anyone would have guessed for me in that yearbook.

Buck didn't seem to find the humor in my comment. Not that he was extremely serious, but Buck wasn't the type to find much fun in our mutual situation. Contrary to how it's portrayed in the media, any type of prison just flat-out sucks. Yeah, we were in a minimum security facility, but it was no Club Fed. And for Buck – well, he had to earn the right to be here. His first five years of incarceration were spent in a place where no one wants to live. Make no mistake: where we were now was Fed, but the only part of it that was a club was the fact that once we were labeled convicted felons, we would always be convicted felons – a consequence that will last the rest of our lives.

"It's not really funny, Chuck! You always seem to try to find some humor. Don't get me wrong – I like to laugh. But maybe you need to get serious sometimes. Let me ask you. Why do people stray off the straight and narrow? How do you keep them on track? In hindsight, both of us can look at ourselves and see the obvious warning signs, but wouldn't it be cool if we could recognize the warning signs before we made such dumb-ass choices? We could have prevented this chapter of our lives if we had just been aware of what we were doing. Maybe that's just not possible for folks like us."

Buck had struck a chord within me, and just as I was preparing to wax philosophical, we were interrupted by the Thursday night call for prison nachos. Conversation closed, at least for the moment, but its beginning had started a thought process that in many ways continues to this day.

• • •

Either something happened that threw our lives out of balance, or we made stupid choices that moved our lives out of balance. Either way, when life gets out of balance, it's human nature to bring it back into balance, or what we perceive to be balance.

• • •

Over the next several days, the conversation Buck started caused me to ponder more than once. Most of the folks in prison, including Buck and me, could trace our first choices back to an attempt to solve what we perceived to be a need in our lives. Either something happened that threw our lives out of balance, or we made stupid choices that moved our lives out of balance. Either way, when life gets out of balance, it's human nature to bring it back into balance, or what we perceive to be balance.

In an odd sort of way, I was perplexed. The more I thought of tracing back to the source of the dumb choices I'd made that got me to where I was, the more I became aware that the need, or perceived need, alone was not the problem. It certainly was the source of the original choices – just like Adam and Eve. But there was another part of the equation I required in order to move the process of choice and consequence forward. No matter how strong the need, if there's no source or opportunity to satisfy the need, then the need will go unmet, and the challenge will fail. To burn, a fire must have fuel. To satisfy a need, there must be an opportunity. What was so simple and obvious was also quite profound to me, and I couldn't wait to share it with Buck.

The weekend came and went all too fast. Both of us were blessed to have visits. The simple thought that someone would take their time out of their schedule to come to a prison to visit us was thrilling and humbling. After all, it was so easy for most people to forget those of us who, by our choices, were out of sight.

By Sunday night, count time had come and gone, and we began to mentally prepare, like most of society, for a Monday workday. Yes…we were required to work in prison. That night, I could tell Buck had something on his mind. He had a unique way of going silent till he churned through the possibilities in his head before speaking.

"What do you think would have happened, Chuck, if you'd never been the trustee of that trust?"

I'm not sure Buck would have believed me if I told him just how many times I'd asked myself that very question: What if there had never been a trust fund? Better still the question might have been: What if I had been more responsible and not gotten into so much debt in the first place?

"You know, Buck, what-ifs will drive you crazy!"

"That may be true but, really, what if we had never had the opportunity?"

As Buck asked that question, it became clear to me that we both were tuned into the same channel, each without the other knowing it. Opportunity was the second component needed in order for a choice that satisfied a need to have the possibility of becoming a reality. For me, if there hadn't been a trust fund, then I would have had no choice but to solve my problem in a legitimate, legal way. In hindsight, the only correct solution would have been to tell the truth. Dealing with the consequences then would have created a far different outcome now.

For Buck, had there not been a drug dealer who was willing and eager to get him into the business, he'd have had no choice but to do something legitimate. Consider the need (or perceived need) and think about this: If there were no opportunity, then the choices we made would naturally fail. Of course, there always seems to be some sort of opportunity.

"Weird, but we're both thinking the same thing," I said.

"Yeah," replied Buck. "We're not just here in this room by chance. There's something bigger in play, Chuck."

Buck was right, and over the years, as I look back on my writings from prison where I took copious notes of our conversations, it's clear to me that our relationship was not by chance. Buck was there for me, and I for him – in ways that likely neither of us truly realizes even today.

Now some twenty years later, I recognize several "Aha!" moments that have become crystal clear to me. These moments can be quite profound if we apply them to our lives or businesses.

Consider this question: If you asked your employees or family whether they would voluntarily choose to do something unethical or illegal, what do you think they would say? My guess – from years of asking that question – is that they would say "NO!" Yet in a country that has the highest incarceration rate of any developed country, we must conclude that many people, when faced with significant temptation (need), will in fact make choices that don't serve them well.

Think of how the application of a few fundamental principles today can create dramatic change for the good! What if we become more aware of need in other people, recognizing that heightened need creates the desire for a solution, and that desire forces us to seek an opportunity for a solution? Simple, yet profound.

As an employer, I can't control the need that my employees might experience, but I can be aware of it. We

• • •

If you asked your employees or family whether they would voluntarily choose to do something unethical or illegal, what do you think they would say?

• • •

get so caught up trying to control choices in the business world that we lose sight of what motivates our choices in the first place. We think that preparing an ethics and compliance manifesto for employees to sign ensures that they'll make intelligent, ethical, and legal choices. But it doesn't...not even close! One of the most powerful motivators of ethical behavior is being aware of times when life is out of balance. For example, it's possible to be aware that someone's having a problem with debt if they're getting creditor calls all the time. You know what those calls sound like. You know the embarrassment an employee might feel if they're getting harassing creditor calls at work. So when you hear these calls come in and see their frequency, you could – if you're willing to be tuned into the employees on your team – know that life is out of balance and that the need factor is high for that particular employee.

If you're mindful that someone's need factor is climbing, that life is out of balance for them, you may not be able to control or solve their problem, but you can certainly change your struggling employee's work experience to remove the opportunity that would enable this need to be resolved in an unproductive, unethical manner. This could mean providing help with an employee assistance program or offering financial coaching to your employees or staff. Perhaps, hard as it might sound, you go as far as removing financial responsibilities from this person, at least temporarily. Remember – no trust fund for Chuck, no chance of theft.

Needs come in all sizes and situations. Make no mistake – you can experience an out-of-balance life when things go way bad or way good. Just ask yourself how many people who gain a major inheritance or win the lottery end up ten years later with financial challenges. Life out of balance can happen in a number of ways that we as humans experience daily – money, health, relationships, or anything that involves a lawyer or a doctor (just having some fun here). Nevertheless, whatever requires specialized help is likely an indication that an out-of-balance life is seeking balance through some opportunity.

We can't control need in other people's lives. From an employer's perspective, removing opportunity is what an employer has the most control over. Most ethics and compliance courses taught in corporate organizations today are rule-based or fear-based programs. These are the rules, they say, and here are the consequences if you fail to follow them. It's the approach most commonly promoted in business. However, the challenge is that, while it's a powerful motivator, fear doesn't allow an organization to address the real foundation of human behavior – namely what motivates someone to make an unethical choice and what can be done to prevent him or her from doing so.

It makes no difference what the ethics rules or code of conduct say when an employee's life is dramatically out of balance. An out-of-balance life will seek to find balance, and that means – pure and simple – that if the opportunity for an unethical decision is present, there will be a strong temptation for the employee to make it.

Opportunity is not to blame for the incredibly poor choices I made. But opportunity allowed me the opening to make a fatefully bad decision – one that changed my life forever. That's true for all people. If there's no opportunity for unethical behavior, then there's no bad way to meet the need we're trying to fulfill.

The reality is that in trying to make our environment a perfectly safe place, there's no way we can remove all opportunity for unethical behavior. The question, then, is this: Can we be vigilant enough to recognize an out-of-balance life, so that we can close the door on opportunity and reduce the likelihood that someone will gravitate toward poor choices?

A person can be thirty years sober, but it doesn't mean they're not still an alcoholic. They are. They've just been strong for thirty years. They always have to be vigilant and aware of what's taking place around them so they can avoid a tempting environment that could cause them to fall off the wagon. Likewise, those close to the alcoholic would be well advised to remove temptation or opportunity from the equation. That's an act of kindness or love. An employer, spouse, or other person of close connection can assist an alcoholic to stay sober by removing the tempting opportunities with such things as not going to bars for entertainment, not serving alcohol at the company picnic, etc. This is but one example of the many ways we can show caring and compassion for those who have a high need factor in their lives.

Not long ago, a participant in a presentation made to the Montana Society of CPAs asked: Other than you just not making the choice you did, what one thing could have prevented you from making the unethical, illegal choice you made? My response: "Two signatures on the trust check!"

At the risk of sounding unremorseful, which is not at all how I feel, I have to remove the emotion from the situation and take an honest look all the way around at what I did and how it happened. I clearly had a need, which I talked about in detail earlier. It's also clear that an opportunity to solve that need stared me in the face – I had full access to trust funds with no oversight. Stop! You may want to reread that last sentence. I had full access to trust funds with no oversight. Put simply, to clearly answer the gentleman's question, if the trust checks had required two signatures to be valid (most will recognize that as a simple internal control), then I would have had no access to the funds and hence been denied the opportunity.

Removing opportunity isn't rocket science! All it requires, for the most part, is the use of God-given common sense. Yet, you have no idea the number of organizations I'm blessed to consult with and speak to who pay me with a check requiring only one signature. To be clear – most people are honest and would never take money from an organization, but why create the opportunity or temptation when a simple change in procedure could prevent a wrong choice?

Not long ago I was engaged to consult with a company to review their systems and identify places where opportunity for unethical choices could be reduced or eliminated. One of the first things we did was to create a job cross-training program. The idea, on the surface, was to make sure that someone else knew your job and you theirs so that, should someone get sick or need time off, there would be another person who was competent to perform the task. Beneath the surface, however, the added value was to create some discomfort and remove people from roles where they had the opportunity to make bad decisions.

Most employees were receptive to the program. They actually welcomed the change of pace and the new role they'd been assigned. Heck, some viewed it as a way to expand their awareness of the organization and potentially create a path for future advancement. But Rosa, an executive assistant to the vice president of purchasing, was quite resistant, telling her boss that she didn't have time for such foolishness. Over the course of the initial implementation, she and another person created the most noise and roadblocks to the program.

Meeting with the executive team a month in, I told them, "There are many reasons people resist change. After all, change can be especially hard for some. You have to either enforce the program and process, or accept that some employees are going to control the workflow of your company."

• • •

"Living beyond means, financial difficulties, unusually close association with vendors or customers, and excessive control issues are the most commonly observed behavioral warning signs."

• • •

Jack, the chief operating officer, knowing the value of what we were doing, spoke up. "The purpose behind this program is to strengthen our core, develop our employees, and disrupt opportunity. So I have a question: What do you find, Chuck, when employees are this resistant to what we're doing?"

His question was clear, but I wasn't sure he wanted to hear the answer. "More times than not there are key behaviors that, when exhibited, are warning signs of a more serious problem. I have a fundamental concern that there's more to Rosa's resistance than we know."

"And the key warning signs are...?" questioned Marc, the vice president of purchasing.

"Well, most of these are signs of need, but where need exists, you can bet that opportunity is following." I went on to list four warning signs of need. "Living beyond means, financial difficulties, unusually close association with vendors or customers, and excessive control issues are the most commonly observed behavioral warning signs."

Marc's countenance dropped. "She's been with me for almost eleven years, and there's no one who has a closer relationship with our suppliers than Rosa. One of the things I like about her is she lets nothing get past her. She runs a tight ship. Do I have a problem?"

The details are not important...but the outcome is. After Rosa was forced, kicking and screaming, to swap jobs and expand her role as an employee, it took only ten days to uncover a massive embezzlement scheme that, when fully investigated, resulted in well over $2.1 million in losses that otherwise might have gone undetected.

Rosa didn't start out as a dishonest person. But her undetected financial need combined with an opportunity to function unchecked provided fertile ground for what started as simple theft and resulted in a life-changing experience for all involved. Disrupt the status quo, create change, and remove opportunity, and you create quite effective boundaries that keep both honest and dishonest people between the ethical lines.

While some may not want to admit it, we all have the potential to make bad decisions when we're faced with a pressing need and the opportunity to address it. The body's natural response to stress is fight or flight – in that moment it's very, very easy to make a bad call. When the body kicks into fight or flight mode, reasoning in the front part of the brain actually begins to shut down. The moment becomes ruled by fear, panic, and instinct.

People steal food for their starving families not because they're bad people, but because, in their opinion, their needs give them no other choice. Understanding the relationship between need and opportunity can help you understand not only your own choices, but the choices of others.

Since I'm open about my past poor choices concerning the prison experience and the recovery that followed, I've often been asked, "What were you thinking?" The question, even to this day, brings a smile to my face, as I reply, "I wasn't thinking."

In fact, that's the point! Rarely do we think when faced with a substantial life unbalance, whether real or perceived. Rational people think. People who have some

• • •

*While some may not want
to admit it, we all have
the potential to make bad
decisions when we're faced
with a pressing need and the
opportunity to address it.*

• • •

level of control over themselves and their lives – they think. People whose lives are in balance – they think. But make no mistake: reasoning goes out the door when you try to solve a need, and you feel there's no option but to take the easiest opportunity before you.

Buck said it best: "Ya know, Chuck, I'd say we're both pretty smart guys, but we sure weren't thinking in the past or we wouldn't be here."

He was one hundred percent right. We both met our needs by taking advantage of opportunities we should never have chosen. Those choices were ours, just like Rosa's were hers. Yet we all have some responsibility to help create an environment that encourages ethical behavior and deters those who might make the wrong choice. What does your company do to help keep people between the ethical lines? What do you do to reinforce that?

CHAPTER 7

COME ON!
EVERYBODY DOES IT!

RECENTLY, I FACED A GROUP OF FINANCIAL PROFESSIONALS, many with their arms folded, knowing they were required to be in this session of the conference. I asked a simple question: "How many of you would voluntarily do something that's unethical?"

It was no great surprise when no one raised their hand. Actually, I suspected that there was someone who wanted to be a show-off and do so, but the vice president of human resources and compliance was present, so no one dared.

"So here's another question. By a show of hands, how many of you believe that voluntarily breaking the law is

• • •

"But everybody does it!" With her words, the crowd erupted in laughter, and a number of other folks loudly agreed with her. She had no idea how profound her words were!

• • •

unethical?" Almost every hand in the room went up. Again, no great surprise.

Considering that the conference was in North Dakota, and recognizing that most people had driven to the event, I knew the next question would be a safe one to pose. "So how many of you have driven on the interstate highway or freeway in the past two weeks?"

Every hand went up. Well, except for two guys sitting to my right who, by their demeanor, were just refusing to play. By this point, as the hands raised, I could also see some grins emerging on the faces of those who had been stoic when the session began. I don't think they were psychic, but I do think they had a clue where this line of questioning was going.

"And how many of you have voluntarily exceeded the speed limit by more than five to ten miles in your driving recently?" With a bit of laughter, most everyone raised their hand. One young lady sitting near the front burst out, "But everybody does it!" With her words, the crowd erupted in laughter, and a number of other folks loudly agreed with her. She had no idea how profound her words were!

The ice, so to speak, was broken when it became jokingly clear that what we say and what we do sometimes don't quite match. Jan, the lady near the front who had spoken up, shared a truth that many of us take for granted but that nevertheless forms the foundation of how we make choices on a day-to-day basis without giving it much thought. We believe that fundamentally we're ethical and we act ethically. Yet we're quite willing to act unethically, and even break the law, when such actions are socially acceptable.

If you don't believe me, just think about the past. Sixty years ago it was quite common to deny African-Americans the same services that Anglo-Americans took for granted. Was that ethical? Well, today we would most certainly say no. But to that generation, discrimination and segregation were socially acceptable. Many would argue you down that their actions were quite ethical, if not morally justified. Unfortunately, even in a new millennium, there are those who still believe that to be true.

I was talking with a friend recently who shared a story I suspect most parents can relate to when their kids are old enough. My friend's daughter, Dawn, had a fresh new driver's permit and wanted to drive at every available opportunity. Her justification to Dad was, "The more experience I get, the better driver I'll be." Deep down, however, she knew that the more experience she got, the sooner she'd have more freedom to go where she wanted and to be with her friends. But, of course, Dad bought into the "better driver" pitch and put her behind the wheel as often as he could stomach the experience.

One gorgeous day in central Colorado, Dawn is behind the wheel, while Dad is becoming a bit more comfortable with her driving prowess. Of course, that nervous feeling is still eating away at him in his hypersensitive state. Traveling down the highway, he tells his daughter she's driving too slowly. She replies by saying, "Dad, we're going the speed limit." The father recognizes that truth but observes, "But all these cars are passing us like we're standing still. You need to just push it forward a little bit." Then he stops himself and thinks, *What am I really teaching her? Am I teaching her how to drive, or am I teaching her how to drive badly? She was observing the law and doing the right thing. But because it became an uncomfortable situation for me, I wanted her to push forward, basically break the law.*

How often, when you're driving, do you go five or ten miles over the speed limit without really thinking about it because you're "moving with traffic"? But when your son or daughter is driving, you want them to observe the law. You want them to be ethical in their actions but find yourself getting irritated because they're not breaking the law. What do we teach our kids?

The essence of this question brings us to the last leg of the three-legged stool that provides the foundation for all the choices we make in life, and firm footing for those choices that are unethical and potentially illegal. Everyone has the capacity to do unethical things when there's an intense need. People act to increase pleasure or reduce pain. Pain and pleasure can be magnified by our irrational mind, especially when fear and desire come into play. This magnification only increases the intensity of the need.

So many times I've had an audience member ask me, "What were you thinking? Didn't you know that what you were doing was wrong?" Both are legitimate questions. The truth behind the answer is this: I used the incredible power of my mind (and we all have that power) to rationalize a way to make my behavior legitimate so I could sleep at night. I worked to rationalize that my choices were somehow socially acceptable.

You know the story. I don't have to repeat what I did. But in order to make my actions acceptable, I had to come up with a way to convince myself that what I was doing was okay. Think with me for a moment. If I had said to myself, *Chuck, you're going to steal money, and that could send you to prison,* then I wouldn't have moved forward. Instead, my internal dialogue went something like this: *I need money. I have a source for obtaining this money and, after all, I'll pay it back. I'm just borrowing it.* That last line, "I'm just borrowing it," made my actions socially acceptable (at least in my mind) and thereby gave me permission to act unethically without too much discomfort.

Think about it. Change one word, and what's wrong is right. "Chuck, you're stealing money." Wrong! "Chuck, you're borrowing money." Acceptable! Now ask yourself this: What words do your teenage kids use to change the meaning of what you wouldn't approve into something you would?

Heck, that's the whole premise behind the internet app Snapchat. Kids love the app because, despite all they'll tell you, the truth is that it allows them to send something they don't want certain people to see – especially their parents – and it disappears after ten seconds or so. The concept behind the app is: "What you don't know won't hurt ya." That, my friend, is rationalization, and it's the glue that holds together bad choices and, in our minds, makes them right.

We started by asking conference attendees a question: "Would you voluntarily do something unethical?" Yet we quickly find that most people would make small choices to lie, break the law, or otherwise act in some unethical manner as long as they can justify it as being socially acceptable.

Recently I was asked to provide some insight into a situation that caused an elderly lady – a pillar of the community and the backbone of a local church – to make shocking, unethical, and illegal choices. As part of the legal process, people wanted to gain insight into why she

• • •

*Most people would make
small choices to lie, break the
law, or otherwise act in some
unethical manner as long as
they can justify it as being
socially acceptable.*

• • •

would do this. Ethel Faye was the church secretary and had held that position for well over thirty years. Yet within a week she would be sentenced to prison.

Ethel Faye was the woman who could quote the Ten Commandments and knew the Bible backward and forward. Everybody thought Miss Ethel, as she was known, was the foundation of the church. Pastors had come and gone, but Miss Ethel was always there – every time the doors were opened. She knew the history of the church, and if you had asked her, "Would you steal money?" her answer would be, "Of course not. That wouldn't make any sense whatsoever. That's against God's law!"

As long as Miss Ethel's life was in balance, all was in order. The challenge for Ethel Faye, though, was that life can sometimes get out of balance – way out of balance. Her granddaughter was diagnosed with a rare form of cancer, and the FDA had not yet approved the only purported treatment that could work. Now, since the treatment wasn't available in the United States, Miss Ethel knew she could send her granddaughter to the Dominican Republic for treatment, but the cost was going to be in the tens of thousands of dollars, probably closer to six figures. Her life was out of balance, big time. She couldn't face the prospect of her granddaughter being denied potentially life-sustaining treatment. To her, *that* was against God's law.

Systematically, Miss Ethel stole money from the church. Her need: treatment for her granddaughter. The opportunity: her access to funds at church, which she had total control over. The rationalization: "God would want my granddaughter to live. And, as long as I'm alive, I'll be able to repay this." What months earlier, when life was in balance, would have been unthinkable, now became quite acceptable to Miss Ethel.

Of course, every choice has a consequence. Miss Ethel's embezzlement was discovered several years following its beginning. And, yes, her granddaughter received the treatments Miss Ethel so desired. The sad reality was that her granddaughter died before seeing the outcome of her grandmother's actions – a sentence in federal prison.

When they found out about Miss Ethel's embezzlement, members of the church were devastated. How could this happen? And how could it happen right under our noses? Quite a few members left the church having had their trust shattered. When you cut through the layers of the story, the answers to these questions come back to three components, the three components of the three-legged stool: need, opportunity, and rationalization.

Rationalization can be seen in our language with the use of phrases such as, "Yes, but...." When we say such things, it's a sign our brain is going down a different road, sometimes an unethical one. "Everybody does it" is another catchphrase that's a telltale sign we're rationalizing our behavior. "Well, of course I exceed the speed limit a bit – everybody does it." Another way we rationalize through language is to say: "What they don't know won't hurt me" (which, by the way, is the name of a book I'm writing for teens, young adults, and their parents). Even Las Vegas promotes the city based on the concept that you can do whatever you please there because "What happens in Vegas stays in Vegas." By the way, that isn't usually true, but it's quite effective in selling "Sin City."

One might ask, "Why does this happen?" Well, when we have an intense need, we'll often pick the easiest, quickest, and simplest solution. We find the opportunity to solve the problem or meet the need in the most expeditious way possible. We act with what many call our "lizard brains." We don't think (using rational thought). Our instinctual response is often devoid of reason. We just take action to solve our problem or bring life back into balance. So, we don't think rationally about consequences sometimes; they don't even factor in. Rather, we seek to solve whatever is challenging us and rationalize that what we're doing – however unconventional – is acceptable. After all, life must get back into balance, right?

Having 20/20 hindsight doesn't mean that, given the same situation, we wouldn't have made the same decision. In my ethics seminars, I'm often asked, "If you had it to do over again, would you make the same decision?" The answer to that is quite obvious: "Heavens, NO!" The reality, though, is that at the moment you're faced with making a choice that's ethical or unethical, it's possible that with enough temptation and imbalance in life, you could still make the unethical – and in my case – illegal choice. I'm not at all proud of the past choices I've made in life. Those choices have created consequences I'd never dreamed of and that, to this day, still impact my life.

What my choices have taught me, though, have been invaluable. The "Aha!" moment for me when I answer the question about doing it all over again is this: Had it not been for my poor choices, I wouldn't have learned the truth about how and why we act the way we do when making unethical choices. More importantly, I wouldn't have had the opportunity to speak to tens of thousands of people today to help raise ethical awareness.

Looking back, you can punish yourself with *woulda, shoulda, coulda.* But it's more complex than that. When humans are pushed into a corner, often the rational brain gets pushed aside. Why? Because the rational brain can inhibit our ability to make a decision that will immediately result in the decrease of a need. In a kitchen fire, if we stop to consider all of our options, we might burn to death. Our brain's failsafe is that it acts quickly and decisively. But it doesn't always do so smartly. Some people make stupid split-second decisions, which in hindsight they would never have made. I'm one of those people. But I'm not alone.

Two months before his collapse from professional sports, if you had asked Ray Rice, former NFL player for the Baltimore Ravens, "Would you do something that could derail your professional career in the NFL and potentially cost you millions?" his answer would be an emphatic "No!" If you had asked, "Ray, would you intentionally take your fist and knock your fiancée out cold?" Again, the answer would be "No!" Yet in a moment of intense emotion, when he wasn't thinking clearly, Ray Rice did both of those things.

At a hotel in Atlantic City, Ray and his then-fiancée got into an argument. People get in arguments, but this was a heated argument. I mean heated like hot emotion. I can imagine that things got loud and uncomfortable. She was screaming at him; he was hollering back at her. But, walking down the hall in a public place, they had to suppress some of those overblown emotions. I mean, you just don't typically have a knock-down, drag-out argument in public. With emotions stuffed, there was clearly going to be a tipping point. Then they got on the elevator, a private place, or so they thought. Fight on! The video of their encounter shows more arguing. She cussed him out, then spit in his face. The emotional temperature was rising!

So what was Ray Rice's need? I can imagine his internal dialogue: *I just need for her to shut up. Shut up!* What's his opportunity? As a professional athlete, he lived in a physical world, so he knocked her out. Did he intend to knock her out? I don't think so. I think he intended to physically rattle her to change the energy of the moment. But as you can see from the all-too-public video, it happened at warp speed. So his need was silence, the seeming privacy of the elevator was the opportunity, and the rationalization was something along the lines of: *I've got to shut this woman up, and no one's going to know because I'm on the elevator. I can do something behind the scenes that no one's ever going to know about.* This sort of rationalization, by the way, is the basis of most domestic violence.

Of course when the elevator opened, Ray Rice's fiancée was lying on the floor knocked out cold. He was trying to drag her out when a security guard came along. Now the cat was out of the bag. And if you know anything about cats, when the cat's out of the bag, you can't put the cat back in the bag. The other thing Ray Rice didn't expect was that there are people who actually look at elevator videos and see the things you do in them. It's not always a private place.

It's easy to become convinced that what others don't know won't hurt me. In fact, I've interviewed a number of young people, and a phrase I often hear them using to justify some behavior they know is wrong is "But what they don't know won't hurt me!" The problem with rationalization is that it's a lie! We can convince ourselves that what's wrong is right, but all we're really doing is buying into the lie of the rationalization.

Rationalization comes in many forms. Let's use presidential hopeful John Edwards as an example. He cheated on his wife, even though she was struggling with breast cancer at the time. They appeared to have a strong, supportive marriage, but appearances are often deceiving. What was his need? Perhaps the exercise of power...perhaps it was sex...perhaps it was a deep psychological need to feel adored. I'm not smart enough or close enough to him to speculate, but I do know there was a need that sparked his adultery.

What was John Edwards' opportunity? The answer to that is easy. Rielle Hunter, Edwards' filmmaker, who was hired to document his presidential campaign, had access. On the campaign trail she was capturing Edwards' movements and gaining an intimate view of the presidential hopeful. Of course, few knew just how intimate that had become.

But the most important question was: How did John Edwards rationalize that? Well, the answer became obvious in the court testimony of the trial that took place. In it, a clear reason rose to the surface: *Men in power cheat. There are certain egotistical and physical needs men in power have. Maybe there's even an emotional need. Filling those needs is clearly important, thus men in power cheat. That's just the way it is!*

That's the rationalization John Edwards used. Ironically, he had a major supporter named Bunny (Rachel Lambert Mellon) who believed the same thing. She was a woman willing to give large sums of money to support him. If you rationalize something, and then you find external support for what you've rationalized, you start to believe your own lies are real.

For her part, Bunny had to get past the person who was in charge of managing her money, so she wrote her donations down as furniture sales. She had checks written for a table costing $1.2 million and other things like that. She knew it was breaking the law, but Bunny reasoned that she was eighty-eight years old and no one would go after her. She was rationalizing: "I want this man to be in power. I don't care if I'm breaking the law."

Bunny said she wanted somebody of Edwards' caliber in office. She felt Edwards was like a new Kennedy, and she was willing to do whatever was necessary to get him in office. That was the mission she felt needed to be fulfilled before she died. It was as if she said, "Before I check out, here's my chance in history to do something that causes me to remember Camelot. That one brief shining moment called Camelot." There was an emotional gain Bunny was getting out of supporting Edwards, but it wasn't from saying, "I think he's a man of integrity."

Edwards had people with a lot of money, like Bunny, assuring him, "It's okay. We're going to help you. We're going to cover this up for you." They had a need – to get him elected. Then they rationalized ways of trying to make that happen.

• • •

The combination of the three forces – need, opportunity, and rationalization – creates a solid platform for potential unethical behavior.

• • •

The problem with rationalization is that no one wins. At Bunny Mellon's funeral, at Trinity Episcopal Church in Upperville, Virginia, Edwards and his daughter Cate were barred from entering. So claims a source connected to the Mellon family. While the service was open to the public, Edwards was not welcome. The outcome of unethical and often illegal choices is a wake of heartache and devastation. No one wins!

By this point, it has to be clear that the combination of the three forces – need, opportunity, and rationalization – creates a solid platform for potential unethical behavior. To be clear, just because all three exist doesn't mean that people naturally choose to make unethical choices.

But we're programmed in so many ways (especially in western culture) to "get ahead" or "throw caution to the wind and go for it." The question – a tough one for so many in senior management within an organization – is: What are we going to do to recognize rationalization and to help people see it for what it is – a destructive force that typically leads to disastrous outcomes?

If you live in an environment where what you're doing seems to be acceptable or the norm, it becomes easier to rationalize. The challenge, whether in business or in our personal lives, is to be conscious enough of our choices to ask ourselves if the three-legged stool is operating in our decision-making process. Likewise, especially for those in leadership positions, another question is: What can I do to help raise conscious awareness of the components required for employees to make ethical or unethical decisions?

Buck challenged me to think on those things. Now I'm challenging you.

CHAPTER 8

BETWEEN THE LINES!

HAVE YOU EVER HAD ONE OF THOSE MOMENTS? Those moments when you get the crap scared right out of you? I call them a "Depends" kind of moment. All right, I know that's a strange question, but there's a connection. I promise.

Several months ago, I was traveling back to my home in Greenville, South Carolina, from the Charlotte airport, a drive I have made so many times I think I could do it in my sleep, or maybe with a self-driving Tesla. It was early evening in the late summer, so there was still a reasonable amount of daylight left, and traffic was moving nicely along Interstate 85 South.

Ahead I began to notice that cars cruising along in the left lane of the interstate had started moving quickly over into the right lane. The movement was odd. After the fairly large SUV in front of me abruptly swerved right, I quickly saw what all the ruckus was about. Seems an eighteen-wheeler tandem truck – FedEx, I think – was swerving and had apparently lost full control. It threatened to cross the interstate median and career into oncoming traffic headed south. That was my lane!

I'm not sure I can adequately do this image justice with words. A tractor-trailer headed into the center of the road, moving in your direction – it's one of those mind-numbing, get-the-hell-out-of-the-way kind of sensations. The only thing separating the out-of-control truck and folks driving in my direction was a series of metal posts with what appeared to be flimsy steel wires that created a barrier. Sorry, but big truck versus little wires seemed to be quite the mismatch. Traffic in my lane began to scatter like wasps whose nest had just been rattled. Frankly, it was amazing that we weren't crashing into each other, as we all tried to avoid the most certain collision that was moving in our direction.

When the dust settled, and there was a crash, it appeared that the metal stakes with wire attached did exactly what they were designed to do – keep the oncoming, out-of-control vehicle on its side of the road where it belonged. Needless to say, there were packages scattered for well over a hundred yards that didn't make it to their destinations overnight. While I'm sorry for their intended recipients, I was glad for me that it wasn't any more than a "Depends" kind of moment.

Question: What the heck does that have to do with anything we've discussed thus far? Let's think about that.

Over the subsequent several days, as I told that story to a number of people, one of my coworkers said, rather matter-of-factly, "Well, isn't that what those things were designed for? To keep people between the lines?" She was right! The State of South Carolina had elected, at substantial expense, to make two significant changes to the interstate highway system within the state. First, they created barriers in the median of the highway to prevent, to the extent possible, oncoming traffic from errantly veering across the center lane and endangering oncoming motorists. Second, rumble strips were etched into the right side of the highway so that if a motorist became a bit drowsy and drifted right, they would be jarred as they hit the strips. The rumble strips not only create quite the vibration, but also quite the noise.

It took awhile, but the evidence was clear. The State of South Carolina wanted, through the creation of an effective system, to keep people between the lines. The culture of the state and its desire for automotive safety meant they were willing to put systems in place that supported their intent – safety. The cost, I'm sure, was significant, but the desire to keep people as safe as possible was worth the cost.

In our daily lives, we can't control what other individuals do. But ask yourself this: Are you making the choices to put the systems in place to keep those you care about, either

• • •

We can't control what other individuals do. But ask yourself this: Are you making the choices to put the systems in place to keep those you care about, either in your family or in your business, between the lines?

• • •

in your family or in your business, between the lines? That question is one that seems simple on the surface but has profound implications, both personally and professionally.

On an individual level, most of the time, if you're doing something wrong, it'll collapse under its own weight. My own actions are the perfect example. I had a need and the need continued. It grew based on my bad behavior. As the need was growing, I recognized the opportunity to meet the need. Did I make rational choices? No! In my head, I had to do something about it. I was able to rationalize a solution (ill-gained money) that helped meet the need I had. But eventually, the choices I had made, based upon flawed thinking, created the collapse that was imminent.

What happens, though, when we look beyond the process for making individual decisions and consider the broader question of what organizations can do about dumb choices individuals sometimes make? Better still: What's the culture of a company, and what systems are they putting in place to protect both the company and its employees? Both Volkswagen and Wells Fargo have to be asking those very real questions, as they face the consequences of massive ethical lapses and internal frauds. They are just two of the many companies that, through failure to create adequate systems that keep people between the lines, find themselves dealing with substantial challenges as a result of bad behavior.

My choices form the foundation of the discussion for this book. But if you focus only on my past misdeeds, then you've missed a greater learning opportunity. We can understand what motivates individual behavior – the simplicity of need, opportunity, and rationalization. The broader question is: What can we do about it? What can an organization do or, better still, what can you do within that organization to disrupt the potential for a poor decision-making process, thereby helping to keep people between the ethical lines? Perhaps the perfect word is "disruption." Perhaps we need to stop, think, and rethink!"

I shared a story in the preceding chapter of a father who was teaching his daughter to drive. She was driving the speed limit, but he observed all the other cars speeding past them and started to encourage his daughter to speed up. Then it hit him that he would actually be encouraging illegal behavior. Rather than continuing to compel her to go faster, he took the time to stop, think, and rethink. In his mind, he said, "Wait a minute... stop, drop, and roll... stop, think, and rethink. Is this the behavior I really want to teach my daughter?"

So what are we teaching our employees? Do we ignore seemingly insignificant behavior – behavior that has been deemed socially acceptable? Do we turn a blind eye toward behavior that shouldn't exist but that's giving the organization the short-term results it desires?

I will never forget what happened when I returned home following the collapse of my Ponzi scheme. Telling my wife was the most traumatic experience of my life, and likely hearing it was the same for her. I can't begin to tell you the sadness that memory holds for me. She didn't deserve my actions or the consequences that followed. But my mother-in-law, upon hearing the news, complained loudly that she knew something was wrong. She reacted with justifiable anger at my actions and at me. I don't fault her for her feelings, but I have to say that when she said she knew something was wrong, I was a bit taken aback because she had gladly allowed me to pay half her house payment and never asked where the funds were coming from.

Think about it for a minute. All too often, companies (and for that matter, people) are willing to turn a blind eye to what might be a misstep, or even an illegal action, when there's a direct benefit to them. Of course, when the truth comes to light, people (like my mother-in-law, as well as folks in an organization's leadership positions) often strike a chord of disbelief and disdain for the unethical or illegal action. The central question, however, is this: What did you do in advance to create a system that would have kept tempted people between the ethical lines?

The best example I've seen in a good while was an experience I had with a multinational construction company that had asked me to speak at a major employee conference. They were committed to ethics and thought my perspective might be beneficial. I was honored, of course, and as part of the event I was to have a few minutes to talk with the CEO of the company. Considering in advance what to say, I thought I'd ask him a probing question, one that later created a story that illustrates what a company that has an ethical culture looks like.

As I was introduced to the CEO, I asked, rather matter-of-factly, "What's it like doing business in China?"

• • •

All too often, companies (and for that matter, people) are willing to turn a blind eye to what might be a misstep, or even an illegal action, when there's a direct benefit to them.

• • •

"We don't do business in China," the CEO said with a rather quizzical look. "We decided long ago that it wasn't ethical. But then you know that already," he added, making my embarrassment less painful. "You see, to do what we do in China would require that we pay off officials who would make the decisions or issue the permits, and that's a violation of the Foreign Corrupt Practices Act. And we don't want to break the law!"

A man with principles, I thought, as I appreciated him taking the lead from a poorly thought-out question. You'd think that I'd have done my homework better. Lesson learned: do research before asking a question and looking dumb. But I digress.

The CEO went on to explain. "The other thing that violates our principles is putting our employees in a no-win situation. If we asked a person to gain contracts for us in China, where you have to pay to play, we would be asking them to break the law and violate our ethical principles. That creates undue pressure for an employee and places them in the untenable position of having to do something wrong to meet the company demands. That's just not right! So that's why you're here – to reinforce that message."

While I know that many companies have a desire for ethical behavior and have said so in writing, this is the first CEO I'd met who was that articulate about his beliefs and the extent he was willing to go to make sure he kept his employees between the ethical lines. His example provides a stark contrast to the written words in the Wells Fargo documentation regarding company values and the systems (or lack thereof) that allowed thousands of employees to defraud customers. By no means is Wells Fargo a bad company, but the difference between the construction company and Wells Fargo is apparent in the systems put in place to keep people between the ethical lines, even at the cost of the company's business abroad.

Pull one leg from the three-legged stool and you can't stand on the stool. The CEO quoted above pulled the leg of opportunity from the mix. No opportunity means no chance to meet a need with rationalization. If you're an organization's leader, you know you can't completely control need. If an employee's life gets out of balance financially – whether because of relationships, their health, or some other cause – you can't control those needs or pressures. Likewise, you can't completely control rationalization, although you have more power there than you might think. What you can control is opportunity, and that's where effective systems come into play.

If you knew there was a good chance your son or daughter might get hurt if they participated in an activity that was motivated by peer pressure, would you warn them or remove them from the situation? If you answered yes, then ask yourself if you're likewise willing to create systems to safeguard your employees so they naturally make the right choices. My guess is, hindsight being 20/20, that both Volkswagen and Wells Fargo would rethink their systems, since their lack of effective ones is costing each company far more than they gained from unethical choices employees made.

And that's all I have to say about that!

CHAPTER 9

BUCK'S CHALLENGE

I GET IT. SOME PEOPLE ARE GOING TO THINK MY NEXT COMMENT is going to sound dorky or weird. But Buck was an angel to me.

Never in my wildest dreams would I have envisioned going to prison. No one around me would have pegged me for a future convicted felon. Nor would I have considered, not even for a minute, that my cellmate there – a short, rather portly young man of African-American descent – would be a guiding light in my life.

I've heard it said that some angels come and go. Buck appeared in my life at just the right time. He committed to help me learn to survive by teaching me the lingo and what effective survival looks like in prison. He committed to me. All he wanted in return was for me to help him learn to, as he put it, "speak correctly" so he'd have a chance at getting a real job when he was released.

Buck and I kept our commitments to each other. He taught me Ebonics and what living in another culture looked like. He had my back. Likewise, I helped him get his first job when he got out of prison. We both had a need, and together we created a legal opportunity to gain our second chances, rationalizing that if bad choices put us in prison, then good choices would keep us out. Now, looking back, that's been true for both of us.

While we were still in prison, though, Buck challenged me in a conversation that happened on a cold March evening, as we sat in our cell talking while most of the other inmates were in the TV room. Buck wasn't one to talk just for talking's sake. Rather, when he would say to me, "Let's talk," I knew he had something important on his mind.

"Chuck, I gotta question for ya."

"What's on your mind, Buck? Don't want to hang out in the TV room tonight?"

"You're gonna get out of here before I do, and I want to know something. I want to know what you're gonna do to make a difference."

"What do you mean, Buck?" I asked, though deep down I felt I already knew what he meant.

"Look, you got an education. You had a good life. Okay, you screwed it up, but from being your cellie for six months, you and I know that you know better. So you

• • •

We both had a need, and together we created a legal opportunity to gain our second chances, rationalizing that if bad choices put us in prison, then good choices would keep us out. Now, looking back, that's been true for both of us.

• • •

have everything going for you. So I'm asking you to make a difference. Do something that'll help others avoid being in this hellhole."

As Buck spoke, I could see the emotion behind his comments. He gazed deeply into my eyes, a look I rarely saw, but when I did I knew he was serious. Buck was facing another four years in prison, and while he knew he'd be released soon enough, he felt little hope that life would be dramatically different for him when his release date came. He committed to me that he'd never be back, but his vision of hope for his future was different than his vision of what he saw for mine.

"Chuck, I've watched you. I know your soul, and I know your potential. Don't waste it. Teach others what you've learned. Help them realize the power of their choices. You've said so many times, 'Every choice has a consequence.' Don't forget to tell others that truth. Help them understand how easy it is to wind up in here and, more important, help them know how to avoid it. And when you do this, do one more thing for me."

By this point in our short conversation, I admit I had tears in my eyes – something that happened from time to time in prison, and something you'd rarely show. I knew that, as Buck spoke, he had touched a nerve. This was coming from a place deep within him that meant it was important for him to share.

"Buck, I commit to you that I'll do my best to honor your request, but what is it you want me to do for you? You know I'll do anything. Well, almost," I said with a smile. We both know I wouldn't break the law.

"Chuck, remember our conversations. I know you write every day, keeping notes. Now go over there and write this down. Your notes are a reminder of our past and a way to remember. Now, I'm going to bed. You go write."

With that, Buck turned over in his lower bunk, the same bunk bed we'd shared now for six months or so, and within minutes he was snoring away. Kid had a knack for being able to fall asleep faster than anyone I knew. And as he snored I wrote, to the best of my ability, the conversation we'd just had. Something significant was there. I just wasn't sure what.

More than twenty years has passed since my release from prison. Buck served almost two more years before his release, and I honored my commitment to Buck by helping him land his first job. Officially, convicted felons weren't suppose to have contact with other convicted felons. But with the U.S. having the highest incarceration rate of any developed country, avoiding contact with others who have made mistakes is nearly impossible.

Buck and I kept in contact for a time. Eventually I was promoted and asked to move out of state. Buck's mom had a medical condition that forced them to move, and over time we lost contact. For well over fifteen years I've tried to find Buck. His name was fairly common, and so all my efforts have been in vain. Courthouse records, DMV records, funeral homes, massive internet searches – nothing gives me the first clue of where to find Buck. Me – I'm all over the internet. But Buck remains elusive. One thing I do know is that one day, Buck and I will reconnect. I'm just not sure it'll be in this lifetime.

I started by saying Buck was my angel. I believe that. One day he was there, and several years later he vanished. But I took to heart what Buck asked of me. Buck asked me not to waste the experience. I hope he sees that, while I'm not perfect, I'm doing my best to live up to his expectation.

So now, I have a question of you. Are you willing to learn from my experience? Are you willing to take to heart those simple components of the three-legged stool that allow good people to make dumb choices: need, opportunity, and rationalization? Are you willing to learn how to apply this knowledge in your life for yourself, your family, and your employees? If you're an employer and you're committed to an organization based on a solid ethical foundation, are you willing to develop a culture that allows for systems that help keep people between the ethical lines?

Every choice does have a consequence. You can read this book and do nothing, or you can make empowering choices that can change your life and the lives of those you're connected to.

Buck changed my life. Perhaps there's something in these words that can change yours for the better, too. If so, Buck would be glad. I can just imagine the grin on his face.

WHAT DOES THE FUTURE HOLD?

FROM THE DAY I TOOK TWENTY-THREE PHYSICAL STEPS OUT OF PRISON, I've learned more than I could have ever imagined. What I began to understand in prison – namely, that every choice has a consequence – has hardened into the bedrock of truth in my life. Poor choices I once made over thirty years ago created a consequence I didn't like and didn't enjoy. But now some twenty-plus years following my incarceration, I've found that positive choices can bring amazing consequences.

Never did I dream that I'd travel the world, speaking and writing about my experiences and sharing openly the powerful truth of choices and consequences. Never did I suspect that, through positive choices, the stigma of being a convicted felon could be managed and even turned into a positive message that resonates with many. Never did I consider, so many years before, that simple actions – generally deemed to be insignificant – can be powerful motivators in the lives of others.

You don't have to be a convicted felon to have struggles in life. And, truth be told, you don't have to be behind bars to be in a "life prison" of sorts. All too often, we find ourselves in less than desirable situations – often of our own creation – and wonder if there'll ever be a light at the end of the tunnel. I can tell you there is! You have the power to choose to become a victim or a victor!

• • •

All too often, we find ourselves in less than desirable situations – often of our own creation – and wonder if there'll ever be a light at the end of the tunnel.

• • •

Not long ago, I received a response to a blog post I wrote entitled "We Don't Hire Convicted Felons! Raising the HR Bar's Blog May Change Your Mind!" Here's the comment:

After reading through the many comments and websites regarding felony convictions, I've come to the conclusion that I'm not alone in this struggle.

You claim with hard work any felon can overcome the past. You're a liar....

As many of us know all too well, the mention of a felony is a death sentence. Every company that I've applied at or interviewed for has turned me down for any position.

This morning I had a job offer with a trash company, went through the entire interview process. What I learned is no matter how hard I try not even a trash collection company will hire me.

My felony is over 10 years old. Stop feeding these people false hope. You're doing us all a great injustice.

By the way, I've applied at hundreds of positions only to be told "never mind, we made a mistake...."

I can empathize with how this person feels. I know that overcoming a mistake or series of mistakes can be trying or downright hard. No one said it would be easy. But the truth still remains that every choice has a consequence. And frankly, if you wish to wallow in misery, clinging to self-defeating thinking, then you'll likely become a victim – a place where many find refuge and solace. But that's not what this book is about. It's not what I'm about. I choose victory and, yes, victory is a choice.

If you want to claim the victory that most certainly can be yours, there are some questions you need to ask yourself. These questions are not easy. In fact, they require you to go deep within and move past the external facade that many of us show the world. You have to become brutally honest. But in that honesty lies the seed of your victory and the foundation on which you can build a life to be proud of.

Question One: What have I learned from this issue, challenge, or experience?

This question, answered honestly, is one of the most profound you will ask yourself. This book is one of the many ways I remind myself of what I learned, and it only begins to scratch the surface. For example, I learned through experience what it means when I say, "Every choice has a consequence." Likewise, I learned that there's great power in our words. The simplest word spoken with little thought can change the trajectory of someone's life, good or bad. Buck taught me many lessons, a good number of which are included here. But most importantly, I learned that even the worst of experiences can become the foundation of something great, if only we're willing to learn and share for the benefit of others.

Question Two: How did this experience or situation make my life better?

"Make my life better? Are you kidding?" This was the response I got from a consulting client who was challenged with moving his life forward after some dumb choices.

"Yes, make your life better!" As we talked, it was clear that he was invested in sitting in his "wambulance" and sucking the energy from others who would identify with his plight. Sorry, but that's "stinkin' thinkin'." And while that's most certainly a choice for many, it's not a choice that creates consequences that most people desire.

I'm living proof that positive choices can have extraordinary consequences! Perhaps, as I think on what I've learned over the past twenty years, there's one other significant question: What am I willing to do with all I now know to make my life better? What action will I take?

• • •

*The simplest word spoken
with little thought can
change the trajectory of
someone's life, good or bad.*

• • •

You see, you have the power to create your own destiny. In fact, your past history doesn't create your destiny. Rather, the choices you make today and tomorrow and the next day create the life you're destined to live. I asked as I began this afterword: What does the future hold? While I can't say for sure, one thing I do know is that every choice has a consequence. And if I make positive choices, the future will be outstanding. I can claim that for myself because I have learned it. Now it's time for you to claim that for yourself!

ABOUT THE AUTHOR

CHUCK GALLAGHER LEARNED A LESSON ABOUT ETHICS, CHOICES, AND CONSEQUENCES THE HARD WAY – but now he shares his experience so that others don't have to.

You may have seen Chuck on television or heard him on CNN, CBS, or NPR radio programs. His business insights are sought after for his strong position on ethics and ethical leadership. Chuck's focus is business – but his passion is empowering others. His unique presentations on business ethics clearly demonstrate that he brings something to the platform that isn't often found in typical business speakers. Chuck's personal experience in building businesses and sales teams while leading companies provides a practical and powerful framework for ethical success.

Currently vice president of a national public company and former senior vice president of sales and marketing for a public company, Chuck may have found a sales niche early on in life selling potholders door to door, or convincing folks to fund a record album of his musical performance at age sixteen (and, yes, those were the days when albums were made of vinyl). But it was the school of hard knocks that provided a fertile training ground for Chuck's lessons in success. Described as creative, insightful, captivating, and a person who "connects the dots" between behavior, choices, and success, Chuck gives his clients what they need to turn concepts into actions and actions into results.

In the middle of a rising career, Chuck lost everything because he made some bad choices. He has since rebuilt his career and his life back to one of immense success. With more vulnerability than the average keynoter, Chuck shares with his audiences his life journey, the consequences of his unethical choices, and how life gives you second chances when you make the right choices. In fact, Chuck's first book, *Second Chances: Transforming Adversity into Opportunity,* has received numerous endorsements and has been described as one of those rare books that effectively bridges the gap between personal accountability and business success.

With Chuck, you get an industry professional sharing practical tested and time-proven methods that can enhance personal and professional performance. What Chuck shares in his presentations – whether training, keynotes, or consulting – is not only knowledge of how to be ethical, but also an understanding of what motivates behavior that can create personal and professional success.

On a nationwide basis, Chuck has helped countless individuals on their journey to success! And he's happy to talk to you. Chuck can be reached via email at chuck@chuckgallagher.com or via phone at 828.244.1400. If you'd like to consider having Chuck present to your organization, feel free to give him a call. He'd love to talk with you.

■

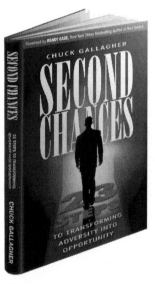

This book, called an "Inspirational self-help masterpiece," was written over the scope of many years and through the experience of many hard lessons learned. I hope that through this book you too may uncover the keys to unlock your prison and find a happier life. You have the power to unlock those chains that bind you and turn adversity into opportunity. You have the power of choice.

Each choice we make and each step we take provide the foundation for our future. Every choice has a consequence. Wherever you are right now, regardless of the circumstance, you can turn adversity into opportunity. Join me, through **SECOND CHANCES**, and let's take the journey together. Now is the time, and the power is yours!

Amazon Reviews

"I bought this book for my son to read while he was in jail. Unfortunately, I don't know if he will ever read it, but I did. Everything this guys says is so right on. I feel that they should make this a reading requirement in high schools. It will appeal to anyone who has faced adversity. READ IT!"

"A must read!!! He has touched my life through the open and emotional sharing of his experience. Chuck Gallagher is a compelling author using his personal experience of wrong choices resulting in negative consequences and how he was able to transform that experience into opportunity beyond belief. This book is applicable personally and professionally. I highly recommend this book to anyone who desires to move past their self-imposed prisons."

"It's easy to see why Chuck Gallagher is sought after as a motivational speaker. He not only has a powerful message. He conveys it in a powerful way."

visit **chuckgallagher.com** today

Made in the USA
Lexington, KY
01 November 2019

56391412R00083